MAKING CHOICES: A PERSONAL LOOK AT ALCOHOL AND DRUG USE

2nd Edition

Sandra Crouse Quinn, Ph.D.

and

Marjorie E. Scaffa, Ph.D., OTR

In Memory of Robert A. Swift, M.Ed.

with special contributions by Janice K. Ruffini, MPH, CHES

OVERVIEW

This workbook focuses on self-assessment and personal exploration exercises, structured to examine knowledge, attitudes, and behaviors related to alcohol and other drug use on three levels. The first level addresses personal issues, such as what students think, what they believe, how they feel, and what they do, relative to their personal alcohol and drug use. The second level addresses concerns relative to family members and friends, such as the impact of an addicted parent on the family, how to identify chemical dependence in a family member or friend, and what to do if someone close to the student needs help. The third level addresses alcohol and drug issues on the college campus itself, in the local community, and in society at large.

Each level has two sections. The first section is made up of assessments that force students to evaluate their knowledge, attitudes, and behavior. The second section follows up with skill-building exercises designed to increase awareness and develop attitudes and behaviors conducive to a healthy lifestyle. This two-step approach acknowledges that, in drug and alcohol education, information by itself is insufficient. Behavioral change requires an exploration of affective components and the development of skills.

This workbook, which could serve as a companion to a traditional text in a drug education class, is designed to meet several needs. Due to its emphasis on self-assessment and personal-exploration exercises, it provides an affective learning component to traditionally cognitively oriented classes. For large classes, it also provides an opportunity for interaction and feedback between students and faculty. Finally, this workbook functions as a private and personal outlet for students to discuss their concerns about alcohol and drug use.

TO THE STUDENT

It has been our experience as instructors that when soliciting opinions on how to make a drug and alcohol course more effective, most students have expressed a desire to explore how they *feel* about themselves and alcohol and other drug issues rather than just be provided with the standard information included in most drug textbooks. Thus, we created a workbook that allows you to do precisely that. You may want to consider the following points as you progress through this workbook:

1) It is probably best to use a pencil with most of the exercises in this workbook. Some of them require decision making that can result in a person changing his or her response quite a few times.

2) All answers and scoring instructions are in Section V at the back of the book.

3) Although the workbook could be used by itself, there may be an accompanying textbook that could provide additional insight or answers to questions.

4) Many of the exercises are self-assessments of knowledge, attitudes, and behaviors. These will change over time, so you may want to complete some of the exercises again at a later date to ascertain whether or not your knowledge, attitudes, or behaviors have changed.

5) While this book is intended for use in your classroom, you may want to share some or all of the exercises with your family or friends, when you feel it is appropriate.

When completing the exercises in *Making Choices*, keep in mind that what you learn about yourself is not absolute, but an estimation of your thoughts and feelings about yourself and how these influence the use of alcohol and other drugs in your life. We hope you will use the information you acquire to enhance and support what you already know or to spark you to take further action if you feel it is warranted. Above all, just remember: the choices you make are your own!

TO THE INSTRUCTOR

It has been our experience that many students who choose to enroll in an elective alcohol and drug course do so for personal reasons. Typically, a fair percentage are experimenting with drugs, and most are drinking frequently, often to excess. In addition, a large number of students are dealing with the substance abuse or dependence of a close friend or family member. For these reasons, we strongly believe that an affective component to traditionally cognitively oriented college drug and alcohol classes is essential. This workbook is an attempt to fill that need.

The workbook also fulfills a need for us as instructors. It can function as a needs-assessment tool through which you can determine the class' needs and tailor course content appropriately. It allows for personal, yet private, communication between students and faculty members and can serve as an opportunity to screen students for alcohol and drug-related problems and make appropriate referrals. We have found that the level of disclosure in these exercises is often quite profound. Therefore, it is appropriate and necessary, at the outset, to assure students of their confidentiality and the availability and willingness of the instructor to discuss these issues in private, should the student so desire.

Many of the exercises may be useful in stimulating small-group discussions, and in some cases, class means and ranges can be calculated so students can find out where they stand on various issues with respect to their peers.

We hope this workbook enhances your students' understanding and ability to effectively deal with alcohol and other drug problems on a personal level, in relationships, and on a societal level. We also hope this workbook enhances your ability to communicate with your students in a more meaningful way about these issues and that you derive satisfaction from knowing you have provided them with more than just facts and information.

If you have any questions or concerns about the use of this workbook, suggestions on future revisions, or want to share your successes with us, please do not hesitate to contact us. We would be delighted to hear from you. Good Luck!

McGraw-Hill Higher Education
*A Division of The **McGraw-Hill** Companies*

MAKING CHOICES: A PERSONAL LOOK AT ALCOHOL AND DRUG USE, SECOND EDITION

(logo) This book is printed on recycled, acid-free paper containing 10% postconsumer waste.

1 2 3 4 5 6 7 8 9 0 QPD/QPD 0 9 8 7 6 5 4 3 2 1 0

ISBN 0–697–22323–X

Vice president and editorial director: *Kevin T. Kane*
Publisher: *Edward E. Bartell*
Editorial assistant: *Kristine K. Fisher*
Senior marketing manager: *Pamela S. Cooper*
Project manager: *Susan J. Brusch*
Production supervisor: *Enboge Chong*
Coordinator of freelance design: *Rick Noel*
Senior photo research coordinator: *Carrie K. Burger*
Typeface: *10/12 Times Roman*
Printer: *Quebecor Printing Book Group/Dubuque, IA*

Cover: *Welch Design Group, Inc.*
Photographs: *from Digital Stock CDs, categories: Sports, Fitness and Education*

www.mhhe.com

TABLE OF CONTENTS

WHAT IS YOUR DRUG AND ALCOHOL IQ?

How aware are you of your feelings regarding your own alcohol and drug use?

At present, many people feel that our society is in the midst of a drug epidemic. At the very least, drug and alcohol use — whether legal or not — has become a rather commonplace occurrence in our society. Before assessing alcohol and drug use on a societal level, however, one needs to examine personal knowledge, attitudes, beliefs, and use of licit as well as illicit drugs.

This first section of the workbook takes a look at personal issues surrounding alcohol and drug use at the individual level. No right or wrong beliefs are proclaimed; rather, we encourage you to formulate your own judgments based on your knowledge, attitudes, and values.

The personal issues segment begins with a self-assessment, first describing the physical effects of alcohol and drugs on the body, followed by facts about alcohol and drug use. Helpful exercises such as the stress checklist and leisure interest checklist will enable you to assess factors leading to substance use. The assessments in this chapter will provide you with a reference point from which to begin further exploration into why and when one uses or abstains from alcohol or other drugs.

From the self-assessment, you can progress into the skill-building exercises, which will help you make decisions about alcohol and drug issues based upon your personal knowledge, attitudes, and values. When making personally relevant decisions, most people feel better about themselves, and this satisfaction is usually apparent in one's actions. Exercises in the skill-building segment range from computing your own blood alcohol concentration to assessing your ability to discriminate between responsible vs. irresponsible use, as well as identifying levels of risk-taking behavior. The latter segment of skill building deals with improving decision-making skills and coping strategies, followed lastly by an exploration of alternative means of getting high.

A PERSONAL PORTRAIT

In today's world, alcohol and drugs present many of us with difficult decisions and challenging situations. Information about their use bombards us from the media, family, friends, school, and health care professionals. However, sometimes our knowledge base may contain myths and misinformation. Our attitudes and beliefs about alcohol and drugs stem from our experiences, values, families, and friends. Yet, we may never identify or articulate our attitudes in a clear way. Finally, our knowledge, attitudes, values, moods, and other factors impact our behavior. For some of us, our behavior may actually conflict with our knowledge about alcohol and drugs and the beliefs we profess to hold.

How high is my level of knowledge about alcohol and other drugs?

What attitudes and values do I hold about alcohol and drugs?

How do I currently use alcohol and drugs?

This growing self-awareness can provide the basis for future decision making regarding alcohol and drug use.

PHYSICAL EFFECTS OF ALCOHOL USE

This test has 20 statements about the possible effects of alcohol use. Put a checkmark to show whether you think each sentence is TRUE or FALSE. If you don't know whether a sentence is true or false, put a checkmark under DON'T KNOW.

TRUE	FALSE	DON'T KNOW	
( )	( )	( )	1. A person cannot get as drunk by drinking beer as one could by drinking hard liquor.
( )	( )	( )	2. Frequent drinkers need less alcohol to get drunk than occasional drinkers.
( )	( )	( )	3. Males can become sexually impotent as a result of regular heavy drinking.
( )	( )	( )	4. Most people would be considered legally drunk after having four drinks in an hour.
( )	( )	( )	5. Heavy drinking over a long period of time destroys brain cells.
( )	( )	( )	6. Alcohol mixed with carbonated soda is less intoxicating than drinking the same amount of alcohol straight.
( )	( )	( )	7. The effects of alcohol will be the same whether or not a person eats food before drinking.
( )	( )	( )	8. A person's chance of developing cancer is not affected by drinking.
( )	( )	( )	9. Frequent heavy drinking often leads to stomach problems.
( )	( )	( )	10. Regular heavy drinking increases a person's chance of developing heart disease.
( )	( )	( )	11. Drinking alcohol slows down parts of the brain.
( )	( )	( )	12. A pregnant woman who drinks is as likely to have a healthy baby as a pregnant woman who does not drink.
( )	( )	( )	13. Regular heavy drinking increases a person's chance of developing pneumonia.
( )	( )	( )	14. About 75% of people who drink heavily develop liver problems.
( )	( )	( )	15. Hard liquor has fewer calories than the same amount of a soft drink.
( )	( )	( )	16. Regular heavy drinking increases a person's chance of having a stroke.
( )	( )	( )	17. A person who weighs 150 pounds will get just as high on three drinks as a person who weighs 100 pounds.
( )	( )	( )	18. Drinking coffee is a good way to sober up.
( )	( )	( )	19. A person cannot become as dependent on alcohol as on heroin.
( )	( )	( )	20. Frequent heavy drinking often leads to a shortage of vitamins in the body.

Student: Remember answers and scoring instructions are at the end of the book!

SOURCE: Adapted from *Program Evaluation Handbook: Alcohol Abuse Education* (1988). Centers for Disease Control and the Office of Disease Prevention and Health Promotion, US Department of Health and Human Services.

PHYSICAL CONSEQUENCES OF DRUG USE

This test consists of 15 statements about the consequences of drug use. Put a checkmark to show whether you think each statement is TRUE or FALSE. If you don't know whether a statement is true or false, put a checkmark under DON'T KNOW.

TRUE	FALSE	DON'T KNOW		
( )	( )	( )	1.	Cocaine ("coke" or "crack") can produce feelings of extreme anxiety.
( )	( )	( )	2.	Smoking marijuana ("pot," "grass") does not usually interfere with a person's ability to drive a car.
( )	( )	( )	3.	Over time, marijuana ("pot," "grass") users must often smoke more and more marijuana in order to get high to the same degree.
( )	( )	( )	4.	Using a lot of cocaine ("coke" or "crack") over a short period of time can lead to depression.
( )	( )	( )	5.	Smoking crack (cocaine) cannot produce symptoms of cocaine addiction.
( )	( )	( )	6.	A person must take barbiturates ("downers," "reds") for a long period of time before needing to take a greater quantity of the drug in order to feel the desired effect.
( )	( )	( )	7.	One reaction to smoking marijuana ("pot," "grass") is a feeling of panic.
( )	( )	( )	8.	Heavy marijuana ("pot," "grass") use has no negative effects on the throat or lungs.
( )	( )	( )	9.	Regular, low-dose amphetamine ("uppers," "speed") users can develop a psychological need for the drug.
( )	( )	( )	10.	People who smoke cigarettes inhale about 1,500 chemicals into their lungs.
( )	( )	( )	11.	It is easy for a person to control the effects of PCP ("angel dust").
( )	( )	( )	12.	Sharing drug needles is a common way to get the AIDS virus.
( )	( )	( )	13.	In small doses, alcohol stimulates the brain.
( )	( )	( )	14.	Methaqualone ("quaaludes," "ludes") is safer than other barbiturate drugs ("downers," "reds") because a person cannot become dependent upon it.
( )	( )	( )	15.	Using shared needles to inject drugs can result in serious blood disease.

SOURCE: Adapted from *Program Evaluation Handbook: Drug Abuse Education* (1988). Centers for Disease Control and the Office of Disease Prevention and Health Promotion, US Department of Health and Human Services.

IDEAS ABOUT ALCOHOL USE

The sentences below are about how you might be affected by drinking alcohol. Put a checkmark to show how much you agree or disagree with each sentence.

		Strongly Agree	Agree	Not Sure	Disagree	Strongly Disagree
1.	People enjoy being around me more when I've had a few drinks.	( )	( )	( )	( )	( )
2.	I can have a few drinks without my driving being affected.	( )	( )	( )	( )	( )
3.	Alcohol helps me get through stressful situations.	( )	( )	( )	( )	( )
4.	Drinking changes my personality for the worse.	( )	( )	( )	( )	( )
5.	Drinking regularly could result in my becoming addicted to alcohol.	( )	( )	( )	( )	( )
6.	Drinking alcohol is bad for my health.	( )	( )	( )	( )	( )
7.	I could have family problems if I drank alcohol every day.	( )	( )	( )	( )	( )
8.	I have more fun at social events when I drink.	( )	( )	( )	( )	( )
9.	Alcohol has been a negative influence in my life.	( )	( )	( )	( )	( )
10.	My friendships would be damaged if I drank a lot.	( )	( )	( )	( )	( )
11.	I feel more confident when I drink alcohol.	( )	( )	( )	( )	( )
12.	Drinking alcohol is a good way for me to relax and loosen up.	( )	( )	( )	( )	( )
13.	I would feel ashamed if I drank too much.	( )	( )	( )	( )	( )
14.	I would have problems at work if I drank more than I do now.	( )	( )	( )	( )	( )
15.	I would have lower grades in school if I drank more than I do now.	( )	( )	( )	( )	( )
16.	Drinking is a good way to forget my problems.	( )	( )	( )	( )	( )
17.	It is okay if I get drunk once in awhile.	( )	( )	( )	( )	( )
18.	I feel that driving a car after having a few drinks is a stupid thing to do.	( )	( )	( )	( )	( )
19.	I would feel more popular if I drank alcohol.	( )	( )	( )	( )	( )
20.	Drinking alcohol is a normal part of the college experience.	( )	( )	( )	( )	( )

SOURCE: Adapted from *Program Evaluation Handbook: Alcohol Abuse Education* (1988). Centers for Disease Control and the Office of Disease Prevention and Health Promotion, US Department of Health and Human Services.

IDEAS ABOUT DRUG USE

This survey contains 20 statements about how people might be affected by using illegal drugs. Read each statement, then put a checkmark in the column that best describes the way you feel.

		Strongly Agree	Agree	Not Sure	Disagree	Strongly Disagree
1.	Using drugs every day can lead to dependence on them.	( )	( )	( )	( )	( )
2.	Drug users usually have money problems.	( )	( )	( )	( )	( )
3.	People can use large amounts of marijuana without it hurting their families.	( )	( )	( )	( )	( )
4.	Cocaine users have more friends than other people.	( )	( )	( )	( )	( )
5.	People who regularly smoke marijuana don't really hurt anyone.	( )	( )	( )	( )	( )
6.	Using drugs causes people to lose self-control.	( )	( )	( )	( )	( )
7.	Regular marijuana users damage their health.	( )	( )	( )	( )	( )
8.	Using drugs makes people more creative.	( )	( )	( )	( )	( )
9.	Smoking marijuana is a good way to relax.	( )	( )	( )	( )	( )
10.	Using drugs helps people overcome boredom.	( )	( )	( )	( )	( )
11.	Cocaine improves one's ability to do one's job.	( )	( )	( )	( )	( )
12.	Regular drug users get into trouble with the law.	( )	( )	( )	( )	( )
13.	Regular drug users have a hard time keeping friends.	( )	( )	( )	( )	( )
14.	People who use sleeping pills rarely become dependent upon them.	( )	( )	( )	( )	( )
15.	Using marijuana helps people understand themselves better.	( )	( )	( )	( )	( )
16.	Heavy alcohol use hurts family relationships.	( )	( )	( )	( )	( )
17.	Smoking cigarettes ages a person more quickly.	( )	( )	( )	( )	( )
18.	People can stay perfectly healthy even if they regularly use illegal drugs.	( )	( )	( )	( )	( )
19.	People who use illegal drugs have difficulty carrying out daily tasks.	( )	( )	( )	( )	( )
20.	Smoking cigarettes helps control emotions like anger and frustration.	( )	( )	( )	( )	( )

SOURCE: Adapted from *Program Evaluation Handbook: Drug Abuse Education* (1988). Centers for Disease Control and the Office of Disease Prevention and Health Promotion, US Department of Health and Human Services.

HAVE A DRINK?

This survey describes various situations in which people often feel tempted to drink alcohol. Put a checkmark to show whether or not the situation leads you to want to have a drink.

	Would you have a drink if	Definitely Yes	Probably Yes	Maybe	Probably No	Definitely No
1.	you were eating an enjoyable meal?	( )	( )	( )	( )	( )
2.	you were watching television?	( )	( )	( )	( )	( )
3.	you were visiting friends, some of whom were drinking?	( )	( )	( )	( )	( )
4.	you had just completed a difficult task that had taken you a long time to finish?	( )	( )	( )	( )	( )
5.	you were tense and anxious?	( )	( )	( )	( )	( )
6.	you had just had a big argument with someone in your family?	( )	( )	( )	( )	( )
7.	you were relaxing after a busy day?	( )	( )	( )	( )	( )
8.	you hadn't had a drink in a while and someone offered you one?	( )	( )	( )	( )	( )
9.	you were waiting for a very important phone call that was fifteen minutes late?	( )	( )	( )	( )	( )
10.	you were at a party and someone offered you a drink?	( )	( )	( )	( )	( )
11.	you were at a sporting or entertainment event?	( )	( )	( )	( )	( )
12.	you felt as if you really needed to drink?	( )	( )	( )	( )	( )
13.	you were with a friend who urged you to drink?	( )	( )	( )	( )	( )
14.	you were meeting a few friends in a bar or cocktail lounge?	( )	( )	( )	( )	( )
15.	you were alone and feeling depressed?	( )	( )	( )	( )	( )
16.	you were celebrating a special occasion?	( )	( )	( )	( )	( )
17.	you were doing paperwork such as studying, paying bills, or writing a letter?	( )	( )	( )	( )	( )
18.	you wanted to feel more sophisticated and attractive?	( )	( )	( )	( )	( )
19.	you were bored?	( )	( )	( )	( )	( )
20.	Could you refrain from drinking regardless of the circumstances?	( )	( )	( )	( )	( )

Review your responses to the situations listed previously and answer the following questions:

1. In what situations are you most tempted to drink alcohol and why?

2. In what situations are you least tempted to drink alcohol and why?

3. Some people tend to drink in response to unpleasant emotions, some in response to social pressures, and others as an antidote to boredom. Are there any patterns to your drinking behavior? If yes, what are they?

SOURCE: Adapted from *Program Evaluation Handbook: Alcohol Abuse Education* (1988). Centers for Disease Control and the Office of Disease Prevention and Health Promotion, US Department of Health and Human Services.

WOULD YOU AVOID DRUGS?

Below are 15 situations involving drugs. Read each situation, then put a checkmark in the column that best describes how confident you are that you would avoid using drugs in the situation described.

		Very Confident	Confident	Somewhat Confident	Not Very Confident	Not At All Confident
1.	You are sitting with a group of your friends, and one lights up some marijuana to smoke. After a few people have smoked, the marijuana is passed to you. How confident are you that you would avoid smoking it?	( )	( )	( )	( )	( )
2.	You successfully finish an important school project and decide to celebrate. One of your friends has LSD and says that tripping is a great way to party. How confident are you that you would avoid using it?	( )	( )	( )	( )	( )
3.	A friend for whom you have a lot of respect suggests that you try marijuana and offers to smoke it with you. How confident are you that you would avoid smoking it?	( )	( )	( )	( )	( )
4.	You are feeling very depressed about school. You remember that a friend gave you some amphetamines ("uppers," "speed"). How confident are you that you would avoid taking them?	( )	( )	( )	( )	( )
5.	You must give a presentation in one of your classes. You are very nervous. Your best friend can get a mild tranquilizer (like Valium®) that would calm you down. How confident are you that you would avoid taking it?	( )	( )	( )	( )	( )
6.	You are invited to a friend's house for the weekend. When you arrive, your friend offers you some mushrooms (psilocybin). How confident are you that you would avoid taking them?	( )	( )	( )	( )	( )
7.	Several of your friends decide to smoke marijuana before an evening study session. They say that smoking marijuana will make studying easier. How confident are you that you would avoid smoking it?	( )	( )	( )	( )	( )

		Very Confident	Confident	Somewhat Confident	Not Very Confident	Not At All Confident
8.	A friend of yours knows where to get "ecstasy" (MDMA) and offers to use it with you. You think of this friend as a trustworthy person. How confident are you that you would avoid using it?	( )	( )	( )	( )	( )
9.	Your parents are out for the evening. Your cousin has some marijuana and offers to smoke it with you. You know that your parents won't be home for hours. How confident are you that you would avoid smoking it?	( )	( )	( )	( )	( )
10.	You have sprained your ankle and are in pain. A friend has some prescription pain killers from a similar injury and offers them to you. How confident are you that you would avoid taking them?	( )	( )	( )	( )	( )
11.	A friend who has begun to smoke marijuana seems to be developing a new set of friends and spending much less time with you. Someone suggests that if you smoked marijuana too, you might get to spend more time with your friend. How confident are you that you would avoid smoking it?	( )	( )	( )	( )	( )
12.	You discover some Valium® (tranquilizers) in a drawer at home. No one is around and you are bored. How confident are you that you would avoid taking them?	( )	( )	( )	( )	( )
13.	At a rock concert, the people next to you begin to use various drugs. They offer each drug to you. They are very nice to you and seem to be having a great time. How confident are you that you would avoid using the drugs?	( )	( )	( )	( )	( )
14.	You are at a party, but you're feeling bored. Someone offers you some barbiturates ("downers," "reds"). How confident are you that you would avoid taking them?	( )	( )	( )	( )	( )
15.	You go to a dance club. You meet some people from school who are going outside to use cocaine. They invite you along. How confident are you that you would avoid using it?	( )	( )	( )	( )	( )

Review your responses to the situations listed previously and answer the following questions:

1. What factors influence your level of confidence in avoiding the use of drugs and why?

2. In what way does the type of drug (alcohol vs. marijuana vs. cocaine) influence your motivation and ability to avoid drug use?

3. In what way does the social situation influence your desire and ability to avoid drug use?

SOURCE: Adapted from *Program Evaluation Handbook: Drug Abuse Education* (1988). Centers for Disease Control and the Office of Disease Prevention and Health Promotion, US Department of Health and Human Services.

DRUG DIARY

For each day for two weeks, record every drug you take on the following forms. Include any prescription and over-the-counter drugs as well as alcohol, nicotine, caffeine, and street (illicit) drugs. Record the exact type and amount of the drug taken and the setting in which you took the drug. Also make note of your mood (angry, happy, depressed, bored, etc.) at the time you used the drug. Finally, make note of your stress level at the time using the following level designations: 1. very relaxed; 2. low stress; 3. moderate stress; 4. very stressed. In order for this exercise to be a useful tool, you must be honest.

An example of a completed daily record follows:

DATE: Friday, December 4, 1998

	Type	Amount	Setting/mood	Stress
Prescription	*Birth Control Pill*	*1*	*home*	*1*
Over-the-counter	*Tylenol*	*2*	*school/headache*	*3*
Caffeine	*coffee*	*1 cup*	*home*	*2*
	Pepsi	*16 oz.*	*school-lunch*	*2*
Nicotine	—			
Alcohol	*Beer*	*4*	*party*	*2*
Steroids	—			
Street drugs	—			

DATE:

	Type	Amount	Setting/mood	Stress
Prescription				
Over-the-counter				
Caffeine				
Nicotine				
Alcohol				
Steroids				
Street drugs				

DATE:

	Type	Amount	Setting/mood	Stress
Prescription				
Over-the-counter				
Caffeine				
Nicotine				
Alcohol				
Steroids				
Street drugs				

DATE:

	Type	Amount	Setting/mood	Stress
Prescription				
Over-the-counter				
Caffeine				
Nicotine				
Alcohol				
Steroids				
Street drugs				

DATE:

	Type	Amount	Setting/mood	Stress
Prescription				
Over-the-counter				
Caffeine				
Nicotine				
Alcohol				
Steroids				
Street drugs				

DATE:

	Type	Amount	Setting/mood	Stress
Prescription				
Over-the-counter				
Caffeine				
Nicotine				
Alcohol				
Steroids				
Street drugs				

DATE:

	Type	Amount	Setting/mood	Stress
Prescription				
Over-the-counter				
Caffeine				
Nicotine				
Alcohol				
Steroids				
Street drugs				

DATE:

	Type	Amount	Setting/mood	Stress
Prescription				
Over-the-counter				
Caffeine				
Nicotine				
Alcohol				
Steroids				
Street drugs				

DATE:

	Type	Amount	Setting/mood	Stress
Prescription				
Over-the-counter				
Caffeine				
Nicotine				
Alcohol				
Steroids				
Street drugs				

DRUG DIARY QUESTIONS

1. Did you notice any patterns in your use of drugs? If so, what patterns were evident?

2. Were you surprised about anything you noticed in your drug diary?

3. Are you concerned about your use of any specific drug or drugs? If so, what concerns you about it?

4. Do you consider your use of any particular drug to be excessive? If so, which one(s), and why do you think it is excessive?

5. What, if any, effect did your mood have on your drug use?

6. What, if any, effect did your stress level have on your drug use?

7. Are any of your drug-taking behaviors in need of modification? If so, which ones?

8. How might you modify these drug-taking behaviors?

ASSESS YOUR USE

Read each statement carefully. If it is true for you, place a checkmark in the blank corresponding to that statement.

____ use alcohol or drugs out of curiosity

____ use them occasionally in social settings

____ function well at school and home

____ use alcohol or drugs for pleasure

____ use drugs or drink regularly at social events

____ using makes you feel like one of the group

____ your rebellion is normal adolescent behavior

____ behavior in school remains stable

____ feel like you need to drink or use drugs

____ feel in control

____ use drugs or drink on a daily basis

____ relationships with your family are becoming strained

____ most of your friends do drugs or drink

____ devote less time and attention to school work

____ need to drink or use drugs to feel better

____ have lost control over alcohol and drug use

____ need to drink or use drugs to feel normal

____ have had blackouts

____ have not been taking care of your appearance, health

____ may steal or commit other illegal acts

____ tolerance to alcohol or specific drugs has increased

____ use drugs or drink several times a day

____ deny that you have a problem

____ stop functioning completely at school, may even drop out

____ become very depressed and even contemplate suicide

____ may have withdrawal symptoms if you stop use of alcohol or drugs

____ may blame others for your problems

Now that you have completed the checklist, please answer the following questions:

1. Do you believe this is an accurate assessment of your use? If not, why not?

2. Do your responses on any of these items concern you? If so, how? Do any of the descriptors you checked seem in potential conflict with one another?

3. Are there any behaviors you see as warning signs? If so, which ones and why?

4. Is there anything about your use of alcohol or drugs that you want to change? If so, what is it and how can you go about making the changes?

WHY DO YOU SMOKE?

This test is designed to provide you with a score on each of six factors that describe many people's feelings toward smoking. Three of these factors represent the *positive* feelings people get from smoking. The fourth is the *reduction of negative feelings,* such as a decrease in tension or anxiety. The fifth factor concerns a "craving" for smoking which represents a dependence on cigarettes. The final factor is *habit* smoking, which takes place in an absence of feeling, or when smoking is purely automatic.

Circle the number that most accurately describes how you feel about each statement.

		Always	Frequently	Occasionally	Seldom	Never
A.	I smoke cigarettes to keep myself from slowing down.	5	4	3	2	1
B.	Handling a cigarette is part of the enjoyment of smoking it.	5	4	3	2	1
C.	Smoking cigarettes is pleasant and relaxing.	5	4	3	2	1
D.	I light up a cigarette when I feel angry about something.	5	4	3	2	1
E.	When I have run out of cigarettes I find it almost unbearable until I can get them.	5	4	3	2	1
F.	I smoke cigarettes automatically without even being aware of it.	5	4	3	2	1
G.	I smoke cigarettes to stimulate me, to perk myself up.	5	4	3	2	1
H.	Part of the enjoyment of smoking a cigarette comes from the steps I take to light up.	5	4	3	2	1
I.	I find cigarettes pleasurable.	5	4	3	2	1
J.	When I feel uncomfortable or upset about something, I light up a cigarette.	5	4	3	2	1
K.	I am very much aware of the fact when I am not smoking a cigarette.	5	4	3	2	1
L.	I light up a cigarette without realizing I still have one burning in the ashtray.	5	4	3	2	1
M.	I smoke cigarettes to give me a "lift."	5	4	3	2	1
N.	When I smoke a cigarette, part of the enjoyment is watching the smoke as I exhale it.	5	4	3	2	1
O.	I want a cigarette most when I am comfortable and relaxed.	5	4	3	2	1
P.	When I feel "blue" or want to take my mind off cares and worries, I smoke cigarettes.	5	4	3	2	1
Q.	I get a real gnawing hunger for a cigarette when I haven't smoked for a while.	5	4	3	2	1
R.	I've found a cigarette in my mouth and didn't remember putting it there.	5	4	3	2	1

SOURCE: US Department of Health and Human Services, Public Health Service, Publication No. (CDC) 75-8716

UNDERSTANDING AND MANAGING STRESS

Our natural physical and psychological response to stress is referred to as strain. The 25 items below are examples of typical strain responses. That is, when we are experiencing stress, it is likely that we will respond as described by one or more of these responses listed below. This survey is designed to help you become more aware of your strain response patterns. It is not a complete list, by any means, but should provide a point of departure for further investigation. Examine the following list of typical strain responses to stress. Then, according to how a particular response is true for you, assign a value to each item as follows:

0 = never
1 = infrequently
2 = frequently
3 = regularly

	1.	Eat too much		14.	Think about suicide
	2.	Drink too much alcohol		15.	Become less communicative
	3.	Smoke more than usual		16.	Feel disoriented or overwhelmed
	4.	Feel tense, uptight, fidgety		17.	Difficulty getting up in the morning
	5.	Feel depressed and remorseful		18.	Headaches
	6.	Like myself less		19.	Upset stomach
	7.	Have difficulty going to sleep/staying asleep		20.	Sweaty and/or trembling hands
	8.	Feel restless and unable to concentrate		21.	Underarm perspiration
	9.	Have decreased interest in sex		22.	Shortness of breath and sighing
	10.	Have increased interest in sex		23.	Let things slide
	11.	Loss of appetite		24.	Misdirected anger
	12.	Feel tired/low energy		25.	Feel "unhealthy"
	13.	Feel irritable			
					TOTAL SCORE

Add the points from each item for your total score. If your score is over 30, you probably are experiencing high stress. It might be advisable for you to review the sources of stress in your life and attempt to remove some of them. You may also gain some insights from examining the pattern of your scores (e.g., circle all of your "3" responses and see if they are interrelated).

COPING STRATEGIES

Coping refers to how people respond when faced with stressful situations. By examining our coping behaviors, we can determine how we typically react to stressful situations and how appropriate and healthy our reactions are.

Look at the following list of 40 responses, or coping behaviors, to stressful situations. If the behavior has been a typical reaction for you in a stressful situation, circle YES. If the behavior has not been typical of you, circle NO.

YES	NO	1.	Tried to relax or calm down by doing yoga, relaxation exercises, meditation, or other activities.
YES	NO	2.	Found or renewed faith.
YES	NO	3.	Engaged in an activity at home (e.g., craftwork, playing a musical instrument, painting), in a project at work, or in physical activity (e.g., sports, exercise, heavy work) in order to take my mind off the problem.
YES	NO	4.	Consulted a professional (doctor, psychologist, minister, etc.) for emotional support.
YES	NO	5.	Smoked more than usual.
YES	NO	6.	Resigned myself to the thought that life would be different because of the problem.
YES	NO	7.	Sought and received emotional comfort from members of my family.
YES	NO	8.	Tried to find some hope-sustaining beliefs.
YES	NO	9.	Calmed myself by eating some favorite food or by eating more than usual.
YES	NO	10.	Took action to prepare for dealing with the problem in the future.
YES	NO	11.	Calmed myself by drinking wine, beer, or spirits.
YES	NO	12.	Felt better after expressing anger toward the source of my problem or those responsible.
YES	NO	13.	Prayed and put my problem in God's hands.
YES	NO	14.	Worked to prevent the situation from getting worse by trying to anticipate what else could go wrong.
YES	NO	15.	Tried to take my mind off the problem by watching TV., going to a movie, going shopping, or taking a trip, etc.
YES	NO	16.	Tried to view the problem as a challenge that I might get satisfaction in handling.
YES	NO	17.	Daydreamed or imagined a better time or place, or actively reminisced about times past.
YES	NO	18.	Read a book or magazine article looking for an answer, and searched for any new information that might be helpful.
YES	NO	19.	Relaxed myself by taking tranquilizers, marijuana, etc.
YES	NO	20.	Viewed the problem as less severe by realizing that there were many others in the same situation.
YES	NO	21.	Felt that only time would make a difference and nothing could be done, except wait.
YES	NO	22.	Made the situation seem more tolerable by realizing that things could be worse.
YES	NO	23.	Took out my frustrations on other people.
YES	NO	24.	Tried to get away from the problem for awhile by assuming extra responsibility at work.
YES	NO	25.	Prayed to God for support or strength to handle the problem myself.
YES	NO	26.	Sought and received emotional comfort from friends.
YES	NO	27.	Felt this was another of life's inevitable problems and chalked it up to fate or bad luck.

YES	NO	28.	Cried as a release.
YES	NO	29.	Tried to hang on until the problem resolved itself.
YES	NO	30.	Stayed close to home where I felt supported and needed.
YES	NO	31.	Complained about the problem, because I knew complaining would make me feel better.
YES	NO	32.	Tried to find the humorous aspects of the situation.
YES	NO	33.	Tried to develop alternative or possible solutions by negotiating with others.
YES	NO	34.	Generally adopted a more optimistic view of the problem.
YES	NO	35.	Accepted the hardship because it was meant to be.
YES	NO	36.	Turned to my spiritual beliefs.
YES	NO	37.	Thought over all the possible ways to solve the problem.
YES	NO	38.	Did something reckless or unusual to get the frustration out of my system.
YES	NO	39.	Talked to someone about how I was feeling.
YES	NO	40.	Tried to get away from the problem for awhile by resting or sleeping more that usual.

First, score your work based on the instructions at the end of the book. If you circled yes to at least three items in any one category, this might indicate a pattern in your style of coping strategies. Think about which coping strategies are healthy and which ones are unhealthy, then decide if you may need to adapt or change your style of coping.

Healthy styles of coping:

Unhealthy styles of coping:

Styles I would like to adapt or change (if any):

SOURCE: Adapted from Stone and Neale. (1984). New measure of daily coping: Development and preliminary results. *Journal of Personality and Social Psychology,* 46 (4), 892-906.

ARE YOU A RISK TAKER?

Taking risks is sometimes scary and yet often necessary for emotional, intellectual, social, and physical development. Examine the following questions and respond as to whether or not you would take the risk.

		YES	NO
1.	Do you/would you ride a bicycle without a helmet?		
2.	Do you buckle your seat belt?		
3.	Would you go ocean kayaking?		
4.	Would you go rappelling on rock cliffs?		
5.	Would you cook and serve a new dish for company without testing it at another time?		
6.	If you wrote fiction or poetry, would you show it to others?		
7.	Would you say hello to a stranger on the street?		
8.	Would you go on a blind date?		
9.	Would you take friends to a new, exotic ethnic restaurant?		
10.	Would you play charades at a party?		
11.	Do you dive off the diving board at the pool?		
12.	Would you relocate to a distant city by yourself?		
13.	Would you go to a party when you know you will be a racial minority among invited guests?		
14.	Do you like to take risks?		
15.	Would you lend a friend your car to take on a long trip?		
16.	Would you tell someone that you like him or her very much, if you were uncertain of their reaction?		
17.	Would you ask a friend their honest opinion, even if it might hurt your feelings?		
18.	Do you answer questions in class even if you are unsure if they are correct?		
19.	Would you loan money to a friend if you were doubtful about his or her ability to repay you?		
20.	Would you challenge a professor who you believe is giving incorrect information in class?		

First, score your work based on the instructions at the end of the book. If you responded "yes" to two or more items in any one category, this might indicate a pattern in your risk taking behavior. If you answered "yes" to two or more items in more than two categories, you most likely are a person who enjoys taking a variety of risks.

1. What types of risks are you most likely to take and why?

2. What types of risks are you least likely to take and why?

LEISURE INTEREST CHECKLIST

For each activity listed, place a check in all columns that describe your level of interest in that particular activity.

ACTIVITY	LEVEL OF INTEREST IN THE PAST YEAR			Do you currently participate in this activity?		Do you ever use alcohol/ drugs during this activity?		Would you like to pursue this activity in the future?	
	STRONG	SOME	NO	YES	NO	YES	NO	YES	NO
Gardening/Yardwork									
Sewing/Needlework									
Playing cards									
Church activities									
Walking									
Car repair									
Writing									
Dancing									
Golf									
Football									
Listening to music									
Holiday activities									
Movies									
Speeches/Lectures									
Swimming									
Bowling									
Visiting friends									
Checkers/Chess									
Barbecues									
Reading									
Traveling									
Parties									
Wrestling									
Housecleaning									
Television									
Concerts									
Pottery									
Camping									
Laundry/Ironing									
Table games/Pool									
Home decorating									
Clubs									
Singing									
Clothes									
Hairstyling									
Cycling									
Attending plays									
Bird watching									
Dating									
Auto racing									

ACTIVITY	LEVEL OF INTEREST IN THE PAST YEAR			Do you currently participate in this activity?		Do you ever use alcohol / drugs during this activity?		Would you like to pursue this activity in the future?	
	STRONG	SOME	NO	YES	NO	YES	NO	YES	NO
Home repairs									
Exercise									
Hunting									
Woodworking									
Driving									
Child care									
Tennis									
Cooking/Baking									
Basketball									
Collecting									
Fishing									
Leatherwork									
Shopping									
Photography									
Painting/Drawing									

1. Compare the number of strong interests you have checked and the number of activities in which you currently participate. Is there a large or small gap between these two categories? What does this indicate?

2. Is there any pattern in your leisure interests? Do you tend to prefer physical, social, cultural, creative, or intellectual activities? Do you prefer group or solitary pursuits? Cooperative or competitive activities? Active or passive recreation?

3. To what extent are alcohol and other drugs associated with your leisure/recreational activities?

4. Choose one activity that you indicated an interest in trying in the future. Make the future today and get involved in this activity!

SOURCE: Adapted from Matsutsuyu. (1969). The interest checklist. *American Journal of Occupational Therapy*, 23, 323-328, by Scaffa (1991).

ARE YOU PROTECTED?: RISK AND RESILIENCY FACTORS

Directions: Answer Yes/No depending on whether the statement applies to you personally.

_______ 1. I am academically successful. I have reasonable study habits and get good grades.

_______ 2. I take responsibility for my actions.

_______ 3. I have a strong network of friends who support me.

_______ 4. My friends do not use alcohol or other drugs.

_______ 5. I find it difficult to make decisions and tend to rely on the opinions of others.

_______ 6. I have a close relationship with a parent, teacher, or relative to whom I go for advice.

_______ 7. To me, success means accomplishing something worthwhile academically, athletically, or artistically.

_______ 8. I can easily manage my anger and am rarely impulsive or aggressive.

_______ 9. I get depressed easily.

_______ 10. My home is a place where I feel comfortable and safe.

_______ 11. I am constantly worrying about finances and how I am going to get by.

_______ 12. I go to school full-time and have to work 20 hours or more per week.

_______ 13. At school, I am anonymous and few people would notice if I missed classes regularly.

_______ 14. I consider myself a risk taker as compared to other people my age.

_______ 15. In general, I agree with my parents' values and the expectations they have for me.

First, calculate your score using the answer key in the back of the book. Then, consider these questions.

1. How do you interpret these results? What is your level of risk of developing an alcohol or other drug problem?

2. If you are at risk, can you identify strategies you can use to reduce your risk?

LIFE SATISFACTION QUESTIONNAIRE

Consider how things have been going for you during the last few weeks. Below is a list of things that can influence your happiness and satisfaction with life. Please read each item and indicate how satisfied you have felt about it over the last few weeks. Circle one answer for each.

		Very dissatisfied	Dissatisfied	Mixed	Satisfied	Very satisfied
Over the last few weeks, how satisfied have you felt about:						
1.	Your overall satisfaction with your work (including being a student)	1	2	3	4	5
2.	The amount of income you have	1	2	3	4	5
3.	The physical surroundings and working conditions of your job	1	2	3	4	5
4.	Your overall health	1	2	3	4	5
5.	Your overall physical fitness	1	2	3	4	5
6.	The amount of time you have for doing things you want to do	1	2	3	4	5
7.	What you are accomplishing with your life	1	2	3	4	5
8.	Your ability to change things around you that you don't like	1	2	3	4	5
9.	Your ability to satisfy and meet your needs	1	2	3	4	5
10.	The fullness and completeness of your love/sex life	1	2	3	4	5
11.	Your ability to handle your emotions and feelings	1	2	3	4	5
12.	Your spiritual/religious life	1	2	3	4	5
13.	How honest and sincere other people are with you	1	2	3	4	5
14.	Your general enjoyment of life	1	2	3	4	5
15.	Your standard of living: the things you have, such as housing, car, furniture, recreation, etc.	1	2	3	4	5
16.	The degree of love and acceptance you feel from others	1	2	3	4	5
17.	Your independence and freedom: the chance to do what you want to do	1	2	3	4	5

		Very dissatisfied	Dissatisfied	Mixed	Satisfied	Very satisfied
18.	How you have handled problems that have come up	1	2	3	4	5
19.	Your ability to adjust to changes that come along	1	2	3	4	5
20.	Your ability to get along with other people	1	2	3	4	5
21.	Your close relatives: parents, brothers, sisters, in-laws, etc.	1	2	3	4	5
22.	The things you do and the times you have with friends	1	2	3	4	5
23.	The standards and values in today's society	1	2	3	4	5
24.	Your prospects for a good life in the future	1	2	3	4	5
25.	Your success in getting ahead in the world	1	2	3	4	5
26.	Your ability to concentrate	1	2	3	4	5
27.	Your ability to get things done efficiently	1	2	3	4	5
28.	Your ability to express your ideas to others	1	2	3	4	5
29.	Your ability to share your feelings with persons who are close to you	1	2	3	4	5
30.	Your ability to think things through and come up with good answers	1	2	3	4	5

Calculate your score using the answer key in the back of the book, and consider these questions.

1. Which areas of dissatisfaction in your life can you change?

2. What strategies might you use to increase your overall satisfaction with life?

3. Is your use of alcohol or other drugs related to your level of life satisfaction? If so, how?

SOURCE: US Department of Health and Human Services and National Institute on Drug Abuse. *Research Issue 28. Assessing Marijuana Consequences: Selected Questionnaire Items.* (DHHS Publication No. (ADM) 81-1150). Washington, DC: U. S. Government Printing Office, 1981.

WHERE DO I GO FROM HERE?

After you have completed the self-assessments, you should have a clearer picture of where your strengths and weaknesses lie.

Do you have adequate information on which to base your decisions regarding drug and alcohol use?

How do your attitudes contribute to your decisions to use or not to use alcohol and other drugs?

Is your behavior consistent with your knowledge and attitudes about drug and alcohol use?

The following skill-building section assists you in developing the thought processes and skills necessary to achieve a healthy perspective on drug and alcohol use. Some of the skills include decision making, self-monitoring, coping with stressful situations, assertiveness, and determining your blood alcohol concentration. In addition, this section seeks to help you identify healthy, drug-free recreational alternatives.

KNOW YOUR LIMIT

Drinking and driving is a very serious problem in the United States. It is estimated that between 40 and 50 percent of all traffic fatalities are alcohol-related. In addition, alcohol-related automobile crashes are the leading cause of death for young people between the ages of 16 and 24. Obviously, high school and college age students are particularly vulnerable. How can you tell if you have had too much to drink and should not drive? The following simple formula can give you an estimate of your blood alcohol concentration (BAC). Remember this is only an estimate.

$$\frac{\text{\# of drinks - \# of hours x weight factor}}{100} = \text{BAC}$$

Steps in the Calculation:

1. Count the number of drinks you have had, and subtract the number of hours you have been drinking.

2. Multiply the figure calculated in step 1 by the weight factor. If you are 150 pounds or less, the weight factor is 3. If you are over 150 pounds, the weight factor is 2.

3. Divide this product by 100 to determine your BAC.

In most states, the BAC that constitutes Driving While Intoxicated (DWI) is .10, but some states are in the process of lowering the legal limit to .07 or .08.

If your estimated BAC is .10 or greater, you must not drive. Call a cab, call your parents, or ask a friend to drive you home. It is always best never to drink to the point of intoxication, but if you do, "designate a driver."

Often, when we are drinking, we believe we are functioning normally and are perfectly capable of driving. More often than not, this is untrue, because on a physiological level, alcohol impairs our judgment. Know your limit ahead of time and stick to it!

QUESTIONS

1. If you were at a party for three hours and drank six beers, what would your BAC be?

2. If you were out with a friend and you noticed that he drank five beers and three mixed drinks during the course of a three hour period, would you let him drive home? Why or why not?

3. If you drink, think of a typical situation in which you are drinking. Calculate your BAC based on your usual drinking pattern.

4. If you do not drink, ask a friend to tell you about the average number of drinks he or she would have in a party situation and calculate his or her BAC.

RESPONSIBLE VS. IRRESPONSIBLE ALCOHOL USE

The prevailing societal attitude regarding alcohol consumption is that people should use alcohol responsibly. Yet, how do we define responsible drinking? Indicate whether you consider the following examples responsible or irresponsible and then *describe your reasons for reaching this conclusion.*

1. Ed's girlfriend and family expressed concern over his drinking on Friday and Saturday nights (about eight beers each night). Ed feels he's fine because, after all, "I only drink on weekends, otherwise I'm in control."

2. Four teenagers go swimming together at a nearby pond a half-dozen times over the course of a summer. Each time they take along a case of beer.

3. Mr. and Mrs. Roberts like to drink wine with dinner. They give a little bit to their five-year-old son and eight-year-old daughter.

4. The DMZ fraternity house holds a Saturday night beer blast. Females are allowed to drink as much beer as they want for free. Males are charged 50 cents for each beer.

5. Bill plans on getting drunk at a local bar on Friday night and asks his friend, Kevin, to be a designated driver. Kevin decides it is okay for him to have a couple beers as long as he doesn't drink heavily.

Reflecting back on these scenarios, how did you define responsible drinking? How is irresponsible drinking different? Did those definitions change any from one scenario to the next?

DRAW THE LINE

As much as we would like, the decision whether or not to use drugs is not always clear-cut. There are ambiguities when trying to classify drug use, misuse, and abuse. In certain circumstances, the use of drugs is accepted and even condoned (i.e., taking antibiotics to cure disease, taking Valium® to relieve anxiety). However, in other circumstances, the use of drugs is highly frowned upon (i.e., drinking alcohol then driving an automobile). Have you ever wondered why this is? It is usually an individual decision as to what substances or drugs a person feels are acceptable in a situation. When making these decisions, we are making judgments depending on our values. Values can be shaped by attitudes, beliefs, education, family, and friends. In the following situations, check whether you feel the use of drugs would be acceptable or unacceptable. Then, look again at each item, and check whether you would actually use the drug under the circumstance indicated.

	Acceptable	Unacceptable	Yes, I would use
Taking cough syrup with codeine for a bad cough			
Taking heroin for pain relief in the case of a cancer patient			
Smoking marijuana for better sight in the case of a person with glaucoma			
Drinking coffee to help you get through the day			
Snorting cocaine/smoking crack to help you get through the day			
Drinking coffee to help someone stay up to study for a big exam/finish a big project			
Taking amphetamines to help someone stay up to study for a big exam/finish a big project			
Taking some pills or drinking to help ease the pain of the death of a friend/parent/spouse/child			
Having a drink to relax after a long day at work/school			
Taking some type of drug to avoid thinking about a bad home situation (parents always fighting, getting abused)			
Drinking alcohol to avoid boredom			
Drinking alcohol at meals			
Drinking alcohol with friends at a party			
Smoking marijuana with friends at a party			
Having a cigarette to start your day/after a meal			
Parents smoking cigarettes in front of children			
Parents smoking marijuana in front of children			
Taking aspirin for a headache			
Taking your parent's or a friend's pain medication for a bad headache or other body aches			
Using diet pills to lose weight			
Using something to forget about a bad experience (bad grades, breakup with boyfriend/girlfriend)			
Talking to a friend about his/her drug use			
Talking to a parent about his/her drug use			
Smoking when pregnant			
Drinking small amounts of alcohol when pregnant			
Taking a drink when offered by a parent			
Drinking alcohol at home from parents' supply			
Taking a higher dose than recommended to get rid of bad feelings quicker (an extra tablespoon of Nyquil®, three aspirin instead of two, two Valium® for an extra stressful day)			

QUESTIONS

1. Were there any patterns to your responses?

2. Was there consistency between your attitudes about acceptability and your intention to use the drug under the circumstance described? Under which circumstances did you find any inconsistencies?

3. If you found inconsistency between your attitude and your "behavioral intent" or your indication that you would use under the circumstance, how might you reconcile that inconsistency?

4. What factors influence your decision making when deciding whether or not to use drugs?

WHAT CAUSES YOU STRESS?

Hans Selye, a renowned stress researcher, defined stress as the nonspecific response of the body to any demand made upon it. A stressor, which is an event that triggers the physiological stress response, can be negative (i.e., a traffic ticket or an exam) or positive (i.e., a first date with someone you really like). Typically, the negative stressors are the ones that cause us distress. The following exercise is aimed at assisting you in identifying stressors in different areas of your life and examining how you cope with those stressors. Be as specific and concrete as you can.

1. Identify two academic or class stressors (i.e., the required use of a computer in a class). Be as specific and concrete as possible in your description of the stressors.

   How do you currently cope with each of these stressors?

   Give some thought as to how you could handle each stressor differently. Develop a specific plan for altering your response to one of these stressors. Explain your plan in detail.

2. Identify two stressors in your personal life, such as in relationships with friends/family, career issues, residence hall living, etc. Be as specific and concrete as possible in your description of the stressors.

   How do you currently cope with each of these stressors?

Give some thought as to how you could handle each stressor differently. Develop a specific plan for altering your response to one. Explain your plan in detail.

3. Identify one physical symptom of stress that you experience often. Be as specific and concrete as possible in your description of the stressors.

How do you currently cope with each of these stressors?

Give some thought as to how you could handle each stressor differently. Develop a specific plan for altering your response. Explain your plan in detail.

RISKY SITUATIONS

Examine the following list of situations. Designate the level of risk you perceive to be present in each. In doing so, examine each scenario as an individual entity and do not compare them. After you have designated a level of risk for each scenario, respond to the questions on this and the following page as to how you determined that level of risk.

1 = No Risk

2 = Low Risk

3 = Moderate Risk

4 = Significant Risk

5 = High Risk

____ going home with someone you just met in a bar

____ smoking marijuana in the residence hall

____ riding home in a car with someone who has been drinking

____ trying crack for the first time

____ combining drinking and drug use

____ going to a frat party

____ partying during spring break

____ drinking the night before an exam

____ smoking a pack of cigarettes a day

____ having sex after drinking or using drugs

____ using a false ID to buy alcohol

____ driving a car after smoking marijuana

____ taking an exam while "high"

____ buying drugs from someone you do not know

QUESTIONS

1. How did you define risk?

2. Are there different types of risk?

3. What factors did you consider in that definition?

4. In which scenario would you be more likely to take a significant or high risk ?

5. How can you reduce your level of risk?

DRUG-FREE HIGHS

The desire to experience euphoria or an altered state of consciousness is as natural as sleep according to some experts. The perception of euphoria is influenced by a number of factors and varies from individual to individual. In the space provided, indicate the benefits and the disadvantages to drug-induced euphoria and natural euphoria.

Drug-induced Euphoria

Benefits	Disadvantages
1.	
2.	
3.	

Natural Euphoria

Benefits	Disadvantages
1.	
2.	
3.	

Altered states of consciousness are characterized by a focus on the here and now, a loss of immediate memory, and a transcendence of one's personal boundaries. It is a receptive, sensation-oriented, feeling state. Altered states of consciousness can be induced by bombarding the senses, depriving the senses, or presenting the senses with constant repetition. Typically, activities that produce an altered state of consciousness usually involve one or more of the following:

A. an element of risk, such as skydiving

B. multi-sensory, such as a rock concert

C. timelessness/spacelessness, such as meditation

D. loss of self/ego boundaries, such as a group hug or some spiritual experiences

E. strong emotion, such as fear or love

F. constant rhythm and repetition, such as running

Based on the previous descriptions, list ten drug-free activities that have the potential for inducing euphoria and/or an altered state of consciousness.

1.

2.

3.

4.

5.

6.

7.

8.

9.

10.

DO OTHERS INFLUENCE YOUR DECISIONS? ARE YOU AN INDEPENDENT THINKER?

Most of us are influenced by others when making decisions for ourselves, which is only natural. During the adolescent and young adult years, the influences of others may be especially important. We want to impress friends, yet at the same time we may experience conflict with friends and parents when trying to formulate our own ideas.

The "family and friends" sections will help you determine those who are your primary influences. The exercises in these sections will help you examine how susceptible you are to peer pressure and how assertive you are should you need to resist that peer pressure. You will also have the opportunity to explore the impact of alcohol in dating situations.

We will also examine characteristics of family members within dysfunctional families. The term "dysfunctional family" refers to a family in which someone has a problem with alcohol or some other type of drug. Other factors contribute to dysfunctional families as well.

Finally, there are some exercises, using role-playing and intervention scenarios, that give you a chance to think about what you would do if confronted with a situation where you needed to talk to a friend or family member regarding his or her use of alcohol or other drugs.

RECOGNIZING THE ROLE OF ALCOHOL AND OTHER DRUGS IN OUR RELATIONSHIPS

The use of alcohol and drugs can have a profound impact on our relationships today and in the future. Many of us struggle with being assertive or handling problems with friends that occur even as a routine part of life. Using alcohol and drugs can pose further challenges for relationships between friends, and having a friend develop a problem with alcohol or drugs can be a difficult and trying experience. For those who grew up in homes where alcohol or drug abuse may have been a problem for a parent, awareness of its influence on one's behaviors, self image, and relationships can be very useful.

In this section, you will have the opportunity to explore the role of alcohol and drugs in your relationships with friends and family members. By doing these exercises, you will be able to: (1) recognize how alcohol and drug use, and your beliefs about their use, may have affected you and your relationships, (2) examine your behavior in various situations with friends and family as well as intimate relationships, and (3) assess whether a friend or family member is in trouble with alcohol and drugs. The knowledge you gain through these exercises can provide the basis for changing your behavior and improving your relationships.

FRIENDS

This survey deals with how your friends feel about drug use. Read each statement carefully, then put a checkmark in the most appropriate column.

		All of My Friends	Most of My Friends	Some of My Friends	A Few of My Friends	None of My Friends
1.	How many of your friends would be upset if you took them to a party where drugs were being used?	( )	( )	( )	( )	( )
2.	How many of your friends would think that it was all right for you to use diet pills if you wanted to lose weight?	( )	( )	( )	( )	( )
3.	How many of your friends would be angry if you used marijuana, even if it was the first time you'd tried it?	( )	( )	( )	( )	( )
4.	How many of your friends would be upset if you tried cocaine ("coke" or "crack") just once, to see what it is like?	( )	( )	( )	( )	( )
5.	How many of your friends would disapprove of you having other friends who occasionally use drugs?	( )	( )	( )	( )	( )
6.	How many of your friends would understand if you took a tranquilizer (like Valium®) because you were very nervous about a test?	( )	( )	( )	( )	( )
7.	How many of your friends would be upset if you rode in a car driven by someone who had been drinking alcohol?	( )	( )	( )	( )	( )
8.	How many of your friends would be angry if you got drunk on an important occasion, like a graduation party or New Year's Eve?	( )	( )	( )	( )	( )
9.	How many of your friends consider it normal for students to experiment with drugs?	( )	( )	( )	( )	( )
10.	How many of your friends would take LSD ("acid") with you, if you asked them?	( )	( )	( )	( )	( )

Based on your perceptions of your friends' attitudes toward drug use, answer the following questions:

1. How do your friends' attitudes toward drug use influence your behavior?

2. Do you and your friends have similar attitudes toward drug use? In what ways are they similar, and in what ways do they differ?

3. Do you ever feel unwanted peer pressure from your friends regarding alcohol or drug use? How do you typically handle these situations?

4. Peer pressure is not always negative. Give two examples of "positive" peer pressure.

CIRCLE OF FRIENDS

Friends affect our behavior in a variety of subtle and obvious ways. This exercise is designed to examine their influence on our alcohol and drug use. Here are the directions:

1. Write your name in the center circle.

2. In circle A, write the names of the friends who are closest to you, those with whom you share the strongest relationships, and those friends who are the most important in your life.

3. In circle B, write the names of the friends who are important to you but are not as close to you as those friends listed in circle A.

4. In circle C, write the names of casual friends, those with whom you interact but who are not as important in your life as those listed in the other circles.

5. Now review those names and place a star/asterisk next to the names of those friends who use drugs (including alcohol and tobacco).

6. How do these friends influence your use of drugs (including alcohol and tobacco)?

Circle of Friends

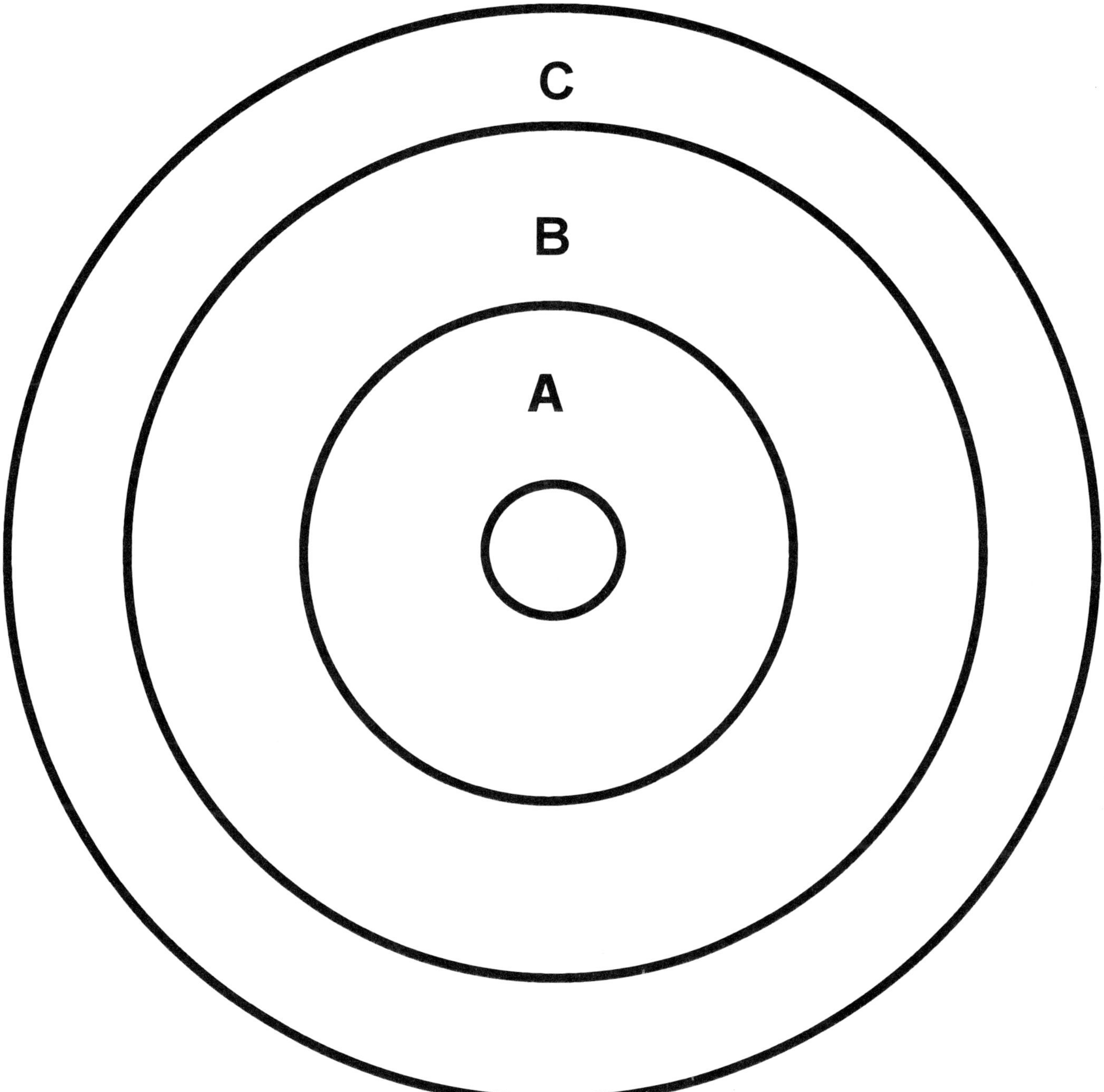

WHAT DO MY PARENTS THINK?

This survey is concerned with how your parents feel about drugs and drug use. Read each statement carefully, then put a checkmark in the appropriate column.

		Definitely Yes	Probably Yes	Uncertain	Probably No	Definitely No
1.	Do your parents believe that it is okay for people your age to drink alcohol on weekends?	( )	( )	( )	( )	( )
2.	Would your parents disapprove of you having friends who occasionally use drugs?	( )	( )	( )	( )	( )
3.	Would your parents strongly discourage you from smoking cigarettes?	( )	( )	( )	( )	( )
4.	Do your parents think that smoking marijuana ("pot," "grass") once in a while is all right?	( )	( )	( )	( )	( )
5.	Would your parents be upset to discover that you had tried marijuana?	( )	( )	( )	( )	( )
6.	Would your parents think that it was okay for you to use diet pills if you wanted to lose weight?	( )	( )	( )	( )	( )
7.	Would your parents be concerned if you took a tranquilizer (like Valium®) because you were very nervous about a test?	( )	( )	( )	( )	( )
8.	Do your parents think that getting drunk once in a while is acceptable for adults?	( )	( )	( )	( )	( )
9.	Would your parents be upset if you rode in a car driven by someone who had been drinking alcohol?	( )	( )	( )	( )	( )
10.	Would your parents be upset if you got drunk on a special occasion, like graduation day or New Year's Eve?	( )	( )	( )	( )	( )

Review your responses to the survey and answer the following questions:

1. Do you notice any inconsistencies in your parents' attitudes toward alcohol and drug use? If yes, please describe.

2. Are your attitudes toward alcohol and drug use similar or dissimilar to your parents'? In what way?

3. In what ways do your parents' attitudes toward alcohol and drug use affect your behavior?

HOW ASSERTIVE ARE YOU?

The items below represent situations in which one can behave in an assertive or non-assertive manner. Place a checkmark in the column that you feel is most appropriate. Answer the questions as honestly as you can in order to learn from your test.

		Always	Usually	Sometimes	Seldom	Never
1.	Do you suppress what you feel?					
2.	Do you keep your opinions to yourself?					
3.	Do you find it difficult to begin a conversation with a stranger?					
4.	Do you find it difficult to express love and affection?					
5.	Is it difficult for you to compliment and praise others?					
6.	Do you admire people who "turn the other cheek"?					
7.	Do "bossy" people intimidate you?					
8.	If a salesman has gone to considerable trouble to show you some merchandise that is not quite suitable, do you have difficulty in saying "no"?					
9.	If you objected, how likely would you be to confront a roommate using drugs in your room?					
10.	Do you keep quiet "for the sake of peace"?					
11.	Would you drive a few extra miles rather than ask a stranger for directions?					
12.	Do you make no protest when someone cuts in front of you in a line?					
13.	If your friend wanted to drive home despite his/her drunkenness, would you confront and/or take action to stop him/her?					
14.	Do you complain to others rather than to those who offend you?					
15.	Would you be very reluctant to return a garment bought a few days previously and that you discover to be faulty?					
16.	Do you find it difficult to contradict a domineering person?					
17.	If someone stole into your parking space would you merely drive on?					
18.	If food is served at a restaurant that is not to your satisfaction, would you eat it without complaint?					
19.	Are you careful to avoid hurting the feelings of others?					
20.	If a friend makes what you consider to be an unreasonable request, do you comply rather than take a stand?					

If you have responded to the majority of items with "always" and "usually," you may not be acting as assertively as you potentially can. However, for items 9 and 13, an "always" or "usually" response indicates assertive behavior. Now, examine your responses for each item and answer the questions on this and the next page.

1. In what situations and with which people are you most likely to be assertive? Why?

2. In what situations and with which people are you least likely to be assertive? Why?

3. What are the obstacles to your assertive behavior in the situations you listed?

4. What kinds of changes can you make in order to be more assertive in these situations?

LOW RISK FACTORS

The National Institute on Alcohol Abuse and Alcoholism summarized the existing literature and found the following factors were indicative of adults who have the fewest problems with alcohol. Which of these factors apply to you? Check the items that apply to you.

_______ 1. You were exposed to alcohol in relatively small quantities early in life by your family or within the context of a religious or cultural group.

_______ 2. Your family members viewed alcohol as a food and consumed small quantities primarily at mealtime.

_______ 3. Your parents set a good example by practicing responsible drinking behaviors.

_______ 4. Your family did not view drinking alcoholic beverages as a means of demonstrating maturity, adulthood, or masculinity/femininity.

_______ 5. Abstinence was accepted as a legitimate choice with respect to the consumption of alcoholic beverages.

_______ 6. Drunkenness was not an acceptable form of behavior.

_______ 7. Alcohol was viewed as a beverage and not as the central focus of a group activity.

_______ 8. The above rules and rituals associated with drinking were known and understood by all group members; they were both reasonable and agreeable to those members.

Score (Number √'d) ___________

The higher your score, the *lower* your risk of developing problems associated with drinking. Based on your score, what is your risk? Why do you believe this to be true?

HOW HEALTHY IS YOUR FAMILY?

Family life takes many forms. Some family characteristics are more functional and healthy than others. A healthy, family environment provides for children's needs in a way that promotes normal emotional, physical, and social development. For each of the following characteristics, circle TRUE or FALSE based on how well they describe your family.

<u>In my family:</u>

1.	All feelings are all right to express.	True	False
2.	All subjects are open to discussion.	True	False
3.	Individual differences are accepted.	True	False
4.	Performance or what you do is more important than who you are.	True	False
5.	Everyone must conform to the dominant person's ideas and values.	True	False
6.	The atmosphere is generally tense.	True	False
7.	Each person is responsible for his/her actions.	True	False
8.	There are clear and flexible rules.	True	False
9.	People feel loved and loving.	True	False
10.	There are lots of "shoulds."	True	False
11.	People feel tired and stressed.	True	False
12.	Growth and change are discouraged.	True	False

Check your answers in the back of the book. Based on your perceptions of your family, answer the following questions:

1. Is your family healthy or unhealthy, functional or dysfunctional? Why or why not?

2. What dysfunctional characteristics are present in your family? How do these affect you personally? How might they be modified?

3. Children of dysfunctional families often become chemically dependent. Why do you think this happens?

ALCOHOL USE AND SEXUALITY

Please read each question and choose the answer you believe is correct.

1. Acquaintance rape most frequently occurs when both the perpetrator and the victim have been drinking. TRUE FALSE

2. Rape is defined as forcing another person to have sexual intercourse of any kind – vaginal, oral, or anal. TRUE FALSE

3. Acquaintance rape is the most common violent crime on college campuses today. TRUE FALSE

4. Eighty percent of college women who have been raped know their attackers. TRUE FALSE

5. Students who drink alcohol and subsequently have sex use condoms at the same rate as students who do not drink. TRUE FALSE

6. Students who drink alcohol and engage in sexual activity are more likely to acquire STDs and/or become pregnant. TRUE FALSE

7. Drinking alcohol increases sexual responsiveness and sexual performance. TRUE FALSE

8. Women and men who consume alcohol are less able to communicate what they want and don't want in terms of sexual activity. TRUE FALSE

Compare your answers to the answer key in section V of this book.

ALCOHOL AND ACQUAINTANCE RAPE: ATTITUDE ASSESSMENT

Please read each question and circle the answer that best describes where you stand on each item.

1. Sometimes men get so turned on with a woman, they just can't stop.

   strongly agree   agree   not sure   disagree   strongly disagree

2. If a man and woman have been touching and fooling around all evening, she must want to have intercourse.

   strongly agree   agree   not sure   disagree   strongly disagree

3. A man can have sex with his date and does not need to get her agreement if they have had sex before.

   strongly agree   agree   not sure   disagree   strongly disagree

4. A woman who goes to a man's room after a party clearly wants to have sex.

   strongly agree   agree   not sure   disagree   strongly disagree

5. If a man spends a lot of money on a date, he is entitled to sex.

   strongly agree   agree   not sure   disagree   strongly disagree

QUESTIONS

Look back on your responses. How do you think people you date would answer these questions?

What myths about sexuality and rape are evident from your answers?

How can you communicate your wishes to your date to prevent harm?

SOURCE: Adapted from *Alcohol and Acquaintance Rape: Strategies to Protect Yourself and Each Other*. The Higher Education Center for Alcohol and Other Drug Prevention, US Dept. of Education, 1996.

READING EACH OTHER'S SIGNALS: PREVENTING DATE RAPE

Read the following scenario and answer the questions.

The party is really starting to rock. Jennifer was excited to meet Tony, a guy in her European History class, and they have been dancing for quite a while. Between dances, they grab a few beers and talk. What a great night it is turning out to be, she thinks. Later on, when the lights dropped and a slow dance came on, Tony pulled her tight against him. A little too tight, and Jennifer pulled back some to create a little space between them. Tony was really excited by her, and bent down to kiss her. A little surprised by the kiss, Jennifer was uncomfortable kissing in public but she did like him. Rather than have him misinterpret her reluctance for not liking him, she just broke the kiss by putting her head down on his shoulder. Tony thought she was just snuggling up to him. Another hour goes by and between the hot room and the beer, Jennifer is feeling a little dizzy. Tony, seeing a chance to be alone with her, suggests going outside for a little air. Jennifer is a little nervous, but really needs to get some fresh air and feel better. Sitting outside on a brick wall, Tony immediately starts kissing Jennifer. Before tonight, he watched her in class, and tonight she has been incredibly sexy. Jennifer wants to slow things down and so she begins talking about her classes. Tony, believing her to just be drunk, keeps kissing her. Jennifer decides she needs to leave, and suggests going back into the party to find her roommate. When they get inside, her roommate has left, and Jennifer, afraid to walk to her dorm by herself, agrees to let Tony walk her home. She likes him but just wants to go home now, and see him another time. When they get to her room, her roommate hasn't returned yet. Tony, believing she wants to be alone with him, opens the door, and when Jennifer says goodnight at the door, he just walks in and makes himself at home on the couch. He suggests she sit down, and feeling a little woozy and tired, she sits down and begins to tell him she is tired and he needs to go home. He begins kissing her again, and reaches for the buttons on her blouse. She turns her head away to avoid kissing him, and tells him, "No, I don't want to. Stop." Tony just thinks she is being coy, and starts pulling off her pants. She finally stopped saying no and began crying when he penetrated her.

1. Name two times when Tony could have been more respectful of Jennifer's feelings.

2. How did Jennifer make herself vulnerable?

3. Date rape often moves through 3 stages:
    - one person intrudes upon another's personal space in a public setting;
    - the other person doesn't conclusively stop that intrusion and the intruder thinks his behavior is acceptable;
    - when the couple is in a more private space, rape occurs.

How could Jennifer have stopped this progress?

What behaviors of Jennifer's at these stages did Tony ignore?

4. How did alcohol influence Tony's behavior? Jennifer's behavior?

WHAT CAN I DO?

Now that you have completed the assessments of how alcohol and other drugs affect your relationships, you should have a better idea of the positive and negative effects of parental alcohol and drug use, and the attitudes and behaviors of friends and family members. Some questions to ask yourself at this point are:

Are my family and friends positive or negative influences in my quest for a healthy lifestyle?

Do my family members and friends have alcohol and drug-related problems, and how do these problems affect me?

What can I do if a family member or friend is in trouble with alcohol and/or other drugs?

This skill-building section attempts to assist you in developing the thought processes and skills necessary to achieve a healthy perspective on the drug and alcohol use of your family and friends. Some of the skills include handling peer pressure, identifying chemical dependence in family members and friends, learning about available resources, and how to intervene when someone you care about needs help.

BECOMING MORE ASSERTIVE

Assertiveness is behavior that enables you to act in your best interests, to stand up for yourself without undue anxiety, to exercise your rights without denying the rights of others. It is the direct, honest, appropriate expression of one's feelings, opinions, or beliefs. It shows consideration, but not deference, for other people. Assertive behavior communicates respect for the other person, but not necessarily the other person's behavior. There are four behavioral components of assertive behavior:

1. Content

   A. In any assertive behavior, some specific goal is involved:

      1) To establish a relationship with someone you want to know, or to change or end a relationship
      2) To express your feelings, beliefs, or opinions.
      3) To state an objection or point of view in opposition to another.
      4) To set limits for another person in regard to what can be expected or demanded of you.
      5) To obtain something you want.

   B. Usually there are three basic components in the content of assertive behavior:

      1) Recognition of the other person's feelings and rights (implicit or explicit)-- "I realize you like . . ."
      2) Expression of your own feelings or rights—"however, I like. . ."
      3) Description of desired action—"therefore, let's . . ."

2. Eye Contact and Facial Expression

   A. The other person is more likely to respond to you if you look him or her in the eye.

   B. Appropriate expression lends credibility to assertion.

3. Body Posture and Movement

   A. The more relaxed you are, the more comfortable you'll feel asserting yourself, and the more successful you'll be.

   B. Turning away from the other person conveys a mixed message.

   C. Lowering your head conveys a mixed message usually.

   D. Appropriate hand gestures lend credibility.

4. Vocal Tone and Quality

   A. A fluid, rhythmic statement conveys more confidence than a low, halting voice.

TYPES OF ASSERTIVE RESPONSES

1. Assertive Talk. Do not let others take advantage of you. Demand your rights. Insist upon being treated with fairness and justice. Examples: "I was here first." "I'd like more coffee, please." "Excuse me, but I have another appointment." "This steak is well-done, and I ordered it medium-rare."

2. Feeling Talk. Express your likes and dislikes spontaneously. Be open and frank about your feelings. Do not bottle up emotions. Answer questions honestly. Examples: "What a marvelous shirt!" "I'm tired as hell." "Since you asked, I much prefer you in another type of outfit."

3. Greeting Talk. Be outgoing and friendly with people whom you would like to know better. Do not avoid people because of shyness or because you do not know what to say. Smile brightly at people. Look and sound pleased to see them. Examples: "Hi, how are you?" "Hello, I haven't seen you in months." "What are you doing with yourself these days?" "How do you like working at ...?" "Taking any good courses?"

4. Disagreeing Passively and Actively. When you disagree with someone do not feign agreement for the sake of keeping peace by smiling, nodding, or paying close attention. Change the topic. Look away. Disagree actively and emotionally when you are sure of your ground.

5. Asking Why. When a person in power or authority asks you to do something that does not sound reasonable or enjoyable to you, ask why you should do it. You are an adult and should not accept authority alone. Request convincing explanations from teachers, relatives, and other authority figures. Make it understood that you will live up to voluntary commitments and be open to reasonable suggestions, but that you are not to be ordered about at anyone's whim.

6. Talking About Oneself. When you have done something worthwhile or interesting, let others know about it. Let people know how you feel about things. Relate your experiences. Do not monopolize conversations, but do not be afraid to bring them around to yourself when it is appropriate.

7. Agreeing with Compliments. Do not depreciate yourself or become flustered when someone compliments you with sincerity. At the very least, offer an equally sincere "thank you," or reward the complimenter by saying, "That's an awfully nice thing to say; I appreciate it." In other words, reward rather than punish others for complimenting you. When appropriate, extend compliments. For example, if someone says, "What a beautiful sweater!" respond, "Isn't it a lovely color? I had a hard time finding it."

8. Avoiding Trying to Justify Opinions. Be reasonable in discussions, but when someone goes out of his or her way to dominate a social interaction by taking issue with any comments you offer, say something like, "Are you always so disagreeable?" or "I have no time to waste arguing with you," or "You seem to have a great deal invested in being right, regardless of what you say, don't you?"

9. Looking People in the Eye. Do not avoid the gaze of others. When you argue, express an opinion, or greet a person, look him/her directly in the eye.

SOME ASSERTIVE SKILLS

The following skills may be helpful to you at times. Choose which skills may be comfortable for you.

1. Broken record - This is a calm, persistent repetition of your feeling or need.

"Could you lend me $50.00?"
"No, I'm not able to loan you the money."
"Please! I really need it!"
"It sounds like you're really desperate for the money, but I'm sorry. I can't help. Are there other possible ways to raise the money?"

By using the "broken record," you can communicate your statement and may be able to work out a compromise that meets the needs of both you and your partner.

2. <u>Fogging</u> - This is acceptance of manipulative criticism by calmly acknowledging to your critic the <u>possibility</u> that there may be some truth in what he/she says. You remain your own judge. The effects of this are: 1) you can hear criticism without getting defensive; 2) the critical person may start listening to you and reduce his/her criticism.

"You didn't seem interested in what I said."
"I can see how you may have gotten that impression."

3. <u>Negative Inquiry</u> - This is the active prompting or soliciting of criticism in order to use the information (if helpful) or to exhaust it (if manipulative). This is also nondefensive and fosters communication.

"I don't like your way of treating students."
"What is it about what I do that bothers you?"

In this example, the person may learn about the impression others have of him or her, or about some mistaken information he/she has been giving out. The feedback may be helpful.

"I'm going out bowling."
"Why don't you stay home?!"
"I don't understand. What is it about my going out that bothers you?"

This gives each person a chance to discuss his or her feelings and possibly reach an understanding. The response of "Why the hell shouldn't I go?" would only result in an argument.

4. <u>Negative Assertion</u> - This is acceptance of your errors and faults (without apologies) by agreeing with constructive or hostile criticism. It enables you to be nondefensive and may reduce the other person's anger.

"You did a lousy typing job."
"Yes, I did make some mistakes."

It is important to remember that you must be the judge of your own behavior, and to avoid passively agreeing with unjust criticism.

5. <u>Free Information</u> - This skill is learning to recognize simple cues given by a person, with whom you are talking, that indicates what is important to him or her. When you pick up a cue, you can ask the person about the subject and even mention your own feelings or experiences related to that subject.

"I just moved here from Philadelphia."
"Oh, what brings you to D.C? How do you like it so far?"

6. <u>Self-Disclosure</u> - This skill involves accepting and initiating discussion of both positive and negative aspects of your personality, lifestyle, behaviors, etc., to enhance social communication.

"I am worried about my ability to do this new job."
"I can understand that. I've felt the same way when I started my last job. Is there something specific that worries you?"

Here, not only have you provided some information about yourself for the other person to pursue, but you have also attempted to learn more about your new acquaintance.

WERE YOU ASSERTIVE?

Being appropriately assertive in any relationship is often difficult. When alcohol or drugs are involved, acting assertively and in your best interest may be challenging. The following scenarios focus on situations that may arise with family or friends. Read each scenario and respond as if you encountered this situation. Then review the components of assertive behavior and skills to determine the assertiveness of your response to the scenario. After you have reviewed your responses, rewrite, using the components and skills, those responses that you feel were not as assertive as you would like them to be.

Scenario #1:

Although no one in your family has a problem with alcohol or drug abuse, alcohol is always served at every family gathering. You are uncomfortable with this and would like to suggest a change. How would you handle this?

Scenario #2:

During semester break, you are bringing home a new girlfriend/boyfriend who is currently in recovery from alcohol abuse. You want to discuss this with your parents before the visit and are concerned they will react poorly to this information. What will you say?

Scenario #3:

You currently live in the dormitory and are the only person of legal drinking age on your floor. Other students in the dorm are always asking you to buy alcohol for them, and usually you will do it. But, lately you are getting tired of this and do not want to buy alcohol for them anymore. What will you do?

Scenario #4:

Spring break is coming soon, and you have been invited to go to the beach with your friends. You have enough money to pay for your trip. However, you haven't been home since Christmas, and your parents feel you should spend your break with the family. You really want to go with your friends, and they are counting on you to help pay expenses. What will you do?

HANDLING PEER PRESSURE

Dealing with our friends and peers is often challenging. While most of us want to be liked, we also have to look out for our own best interests. Sometimes, we encounter situations in which asserting ourselves may put us in conflict with friends. In this exercise, read each scenario and respond to the accompanying questions.

Scenario #1:

You are 21 years old and work in a convenience store that sells beer and wine. No customers are in the store when some friends come in to see you. They are all under the legal drinking age. They want you to sell them some beer. You could get into serious trouble, even lose your job, for selling alcohol to minors, but your friends point out to you that nobody is in the store. What will you do?

Scenario #2:

You and your friends find a wallet with $100 and several credit cards in it. Your friends want to keep the money and return the credit cards, saying the wallet was found with no money. You have strong objections to this and believe everything should be returned. What will you do?

Scenario #3:

You and your roommate, who is your best friend, are driving home from a bar in your roommate's van. You have both been drinking, and your roommate is driving. You are stopped by a police officer. Your roommate is in a panic because he/she was arrested for DWI just two months ago. He/she pleads with you to switch seats before the officer approaches the car. It would be easy to do it, and he/she reminds you that you have never been arrested. What would you do?

Scenario #4:

Some friends are going to a campus rally to protest a new university policy. They are strongly opposed to it. You are in agreement with the policy and do not want to participate in the rally. What would you do?

QUESTIONS

1. Which scenarios were the most challenging for you? What made those scenarios difficult?

2. Are there other situations in which you deal with peer pressure? If so, how do you deal with them?

3. What would you like to change about your responses to your peers?

WHAT WOULD YOU DO IF...

Talking about drugs and drug use is not a difficult task, but doing something about drugs and drug use is more challenging.

What would you do if. . . .

1. Your best friend is using cocaine once or twice a week and frequently asks to borrow money from you to buy cocaine.

2. Your boyfriend/girlfriend is getting drunk three or four times a week and already has one DWI arrest, but continues to drink and drive.

3. You notice that your roommate is doing poorly in school, associates with people who sell drugs, and is becoming very moody.

4. Your girlfriend/boyfriend has been reading numerous magazine articles about "ecstasy" (MDMA) and becomes curious and wants to try it.

5. You arrive home from your sophomore year in college and find that your thirteen-year-old sister has started to smoke marijuana. She asks you not to say anything to your mom or dad, because she knows they would not approve.

6. You arrive home for spring break, and the first night you are home, your father becomes very drunk and begins to yell obscenities at your little sister and beat up on your mother.

ARE YOU TROUBLED BY SOMEONE'S DRINKING?

When we have a relationship with someone who has an alcohol or drug problem, his or her behavior creates tension in the relationship. This exercise, while focusing on alcohol, describes situations and behaviors that can also be the result of drug use. When answering the questions, feel free to substitute drug use, if appropriate. Please place a check in the box of any item that applies to you.

1. Do you worry about how much someone drinks?	
2. Do you have money problems because of someone else's drinking?	
3. Do you tell lies to cover up for someone else's drinking?	
4. Do you feel that if the drinker loved you, he or she would stop drinking to please you?	
5. Do you blame the drinker's behavior on his or her companions?	
6. Are plans frequently upset or canceled or meals delayed because of the drinker?	
7. Do you make threats, such as "If you don't stop drinking, I'll leave you"?	
8. Do you secretly try to smell the drinker's breath?	
9. Are you afraid to upset someone for fear it will set off a drinking bout?	
10. Have you been hurt or embarrassed by a drinker's behavior?	
11. Are holidays and gatherings spoiled because of drinking?	
12. Have you considered calling the police for help in fear of abuse?	
13. Do you search for hidden alcohol?	
14. Do you often ride in a car with a driver who has been drinking?	
15. Have you refused social invitations out of fear or anxiety?	
16. Do you sometimes feel like a failure when you think of the lengths you have gone to control the drinker?	
17. Do you think that if the drinker stopped drinking, your other problems would be solved?	
18. Do you ever threaten to hurt yourself to scare the drinker?	
19. Do you feel angry, confused, or depressed most of the time?	
20. Do you feel there is no one who understands your problems?	

Now that you have completed the checklist, please answer the following questions:

1. If you believe your friend may have a problem, how might you approach him or her about it?

2. Are there any other friends, family members, or significant persons who may be willing to work with you?

3. What kind of reaction do you anticipate?

4. What types of resources are available to you to help you prepare? What kinds of resources are available for your friend?

SOURCE: "Are you troubled by someone's drinking?" ©1998, by Al-Anon Family Group Headquarters, Inc. Reprinted by permission of Al-Anon Family Group Headquarters, Inc.

FIND OUT ABOUT SELF-HELP PROGRAMS

Many people have misconceptions about self-help programs, such as Alcoholics Anonymous (AA). One way for you to evaluate these groups is to attend an **open** meeting. Anyone who is interested in the AA or Narcotics Anonymous (NA) program of recovery is permitted to attend an open meeting. You do not have to be chemically dependent. Do not attempt to attend a **closed** meeting; these are only for individuals who are chemically dependent. Anonymous group meetings are held just about everywhere, including college campuses. To find a meeting in your area, check your telephone directory for local listings and call:

Alcoholics Anonymous (AA) – a recovery program for those addicted to alcohol

Narcotics Anonymous (NA) – for those addicted to other drugs

Al-Anon – for those who are affected by a family member's use of alcohol

Nar-Anon – for those who are affected by a family member's use of other drugs

Adult Children of Alcoholics (ACOA) – for those who grew up in a home with a substance abusing parent

Overeater's Anonymous (OA) – for compulsive overeaters

Gamblers Anonymous – for compulsive gamblers

IMPORTANT NOTE: When you attend a meeting, just listen, **do not** take notes, and be honest about why you are there.

1. What meeting did you attend? (type, location, time)

2. What were your expectations before you went to the meeting?

3. Were your expectations met? Were you surprised by anything you saw or heard?

4. Describe the format/activities that occurred during the meeting.

5. Describe the participants and the topics discussed without compromising their anonymity.

6. These programs are based on the 12 steps of Recovery. Describe these steps.

7. What was your personal reaction to the meeting? What did you think and how did you feel about what you observed?

8. Do you believe that these programs are effective? Why or why not?

WE'RE IN THIS TOGETHER...

How do you define community? Your school, your neighborhood, or your city can be each considered a community. Can whole communities have problems with alcohol and other drugs? Does yours?

In a community, the members are bound together in some way. By virtue of this, communities usually have their own unique needs when it comes to the issues surrounding the use of alcohol and other drugs. Unfortunately, what works in one community will not always work in another, even if they are similar, and new strategies will need to be developed.

In the "Exploring Community Controversies" section, you will examine myths about alcohol and drug use, assess the effects of alcohol and other drugs on society, and explore the effects of media on the issues of alcohol and drug use.

In the second part of this chapter, "Addressing Campus Issues", you will encounter the challenges of developing effective policies and programs on college campuses to address alcohol and drug issues.

EXPLORING COMMUNITY CONTROVERSIES

Alcohol and drugs routinely show up in headlines and media attention these days. In our society, controversy reigns over dealing with the effects of alcohol, penalties for drunk driving, and the potential legalization of currently illicit drugs. Images of alcohol use are ever present in television programming and advertising.

In this section, you will have the opportunity to examine broader societal questions. By doing the exercises, you will be able to: 1) assess your attitudes about controversial issues, 2) explore your own myths about alcohol and drug use, and 3) determine your level of knowledge of alcohol's effects on society. Your increased self knowledge on these relevant issues will assist you when, as a student and a citizen, you are called upon to make personal and political decisions about alcohol and drugs.

THE EFFECTS OF THE USE OF ALCOHOL AND OTHER DRUGS ON SOCIETY

Many times we forget that alcohol and other drug use can not only affect people on an individual level, but on a societal level as well. The following questionnaire assesses what you know about the effects of alcohol and other drugs on society. Circle the correct response to the following 30 questions.

1. About what percentage of American adults have a drinking problem?
   A. 5%
   B. 10%
   C. 30%
   D. Don't Know

2. Which of the following is true about the drinking patterns of men and women?
   A. Men drink more than women.
   B. Men and women drink about the same amount.
   C. Women drink more than men.
   D. Don't know

3. About what percentage of American adults have no more than two drinks each week?
   A. 25%
   B. 65%
   C. 85%
   D. Don't know

4. Which of the following is true about children of problem drinkers?
   A. They are more likely than most other people to become problem drinkers.
   B. They have the same chance as other people of becoming problem drinkers.
   C. They are less likely than most other people to become problem drinkers.
   D. Don't know

5. Of the automobile crashes each year in which someone dies, about what percentage involve alcohol?
   A. 55%
   B. 75%
   C. 90%
   D. Don't know

6. About what proportion of violent crime (such as rape and assault) involves alcohol each year?
   A. Less than one-third
   B. Between one-third and two-thirds
   C. More than two-thirds
   D. Don't know

7. What is the approximate annual cost to society of problems caused by alcohol abuse?
   A. Hundreds of thousands of dollars
   B. Millions of dollars
   C. Billions of dollars
   D. Don't know

8. About what proportion of family violence (physical fighting) involves alcohol each year?
   A. About one-third
   B. About one-half
   C. About two-thirds
   D. Don't know

9. When the legal age for buying alcohol is lowered, what usually happens to the number of alcohol-related automobile crashes in which someone is killed?
   A. There is an increase in the number of fatal alcohol-related crashes.
   B. The number of fatal alcohol-related crashes remains about the same.
   C. There is a decrease in the number of fatal alcohol-related crashes.
   D. Don't know

10. About what percentage of Americans say that alcohol has caused a problem in their family?
   A. 10%
   B. 20%
   C. 30%
   D. Don't know

11. How often do marriages in which one or both partners have a drinking problem end in divorce?
   A. Less often than other marriages
   B. Equally as often as other marriages
   C. More often than other marriages
   D. Don't know

12. How does alcohol abuse compare to other diseases in terms of national health-care costs?
   A. Alcohol abuse is the second most costly medical problem.
   B. Alcohol abuse is the fifth most costly medical problem.
   C. Alcohol abuse is the tenth most costly medical problem.
   D. Don't know

13. On the average, how many times each day does a child in America see people drinking alcoholic beverages on television?
   A. About 3 times a day
   B. About 8 times a day
   C. About 15 times a day
   D. Don't know

14. About what percentage of deaths from all diseases are related to alcohol use each year?
   A. 5%
   B. 10%
   C. 25%
   D. Don't know

15. When the price of alcoholic beverages goes up, what happens to the number of alcohol-related deaths?
   A. The number of deaths decreases.
   B. The number of deaths stays about the same.
   C. The number of deaths increases.
   D. Don't know

16. On the average, how many drinks do most American adults have each week?
   A. Less than 3 drinks
   B. About 5 drinks
   C. More than 10 drinks
   D. Don't know

17. About what proportion of violent crime (such as robbery and murder) involves the use of alcohol each year?
   A. Less than one-third
   B. Between one-third and two-thirds
   C. More than two-thirds
   D. Don't know

18. How do alcohol-related automobile crashes rank as a cause of death among teenagers?
   A. They are the #1 cause of death.
   B. They are the #2 cause of death.
   C. They are the #3 cause of death.
   D. Don't know

19. For every dollar Americans spend on alcoholic beverages, about how much money is spent to repair the damage caused by drinking?
    A. 50 cents
    B. 1 dollar
    C. 2 dollars
    D. Don't know

20. Of women who drink, about what percentage continue to drink while they are pregnant?
    A. 10%
    B. 40%
    C. 60%
    D. Don't know

21. Under a $2.9 million federal drug-fighting grant, members of the Texas National Guard:
    A. dressed up as cactus plants at night along the Mexican border in order to gather data on drug trafficking.
    B. invaded Colombia to destroy cocaine-manufacturing plants.
    C. patrolled the Gulf of Mexico in search of drug smugglers.
    D. were sent to Bolivia to train peasant farmers how to speak English.

22. The annual American market for illicit narcotics is:
    A. approximately equivalent to the federal budget deficit.
    B. twice what US consumers spend for oil.
    C. about half the value of all US currency in circulation.
    D. all of the above

23. The US government spends more than $1 billion per year to stop drugs at our borders. According to the US Coast Guard, what percentage of heroin and cocaine targeted for the United States is stopped at the borders through interdiction efforts?
    A. Approximately 37 percent
    B. Roughly 50 percent
    C. A little over 2 percent
    D. As little as 5 to 7 percent

24. The United States represents 5 percent of the world's total population. What percentage of the world's total volume of cocaine does the US consume?
    A. Approximately 37 percent
    B. Roughly 50 percent
    C. A little over 2 percent
    D. As little as 5 to 7 percent

25. The Surgeon General recently reported that tobacco is as addictive as:
    A. Heroin and cocaine
    B. Microwave popcorn
    C. Ice cream
    D. Soap operas

26. According to information from the US AIDS Commission, a primary reason for the spread of the HIV virus, (from which AIDS may be contracted) among the heterosexual population and newborn babies, is the lack of affordable, available drug-treatment programs for heroin addicts.
    A. True
    B. False

27. Coca, used in cocaine production, is grown at elevations of almost one-mile high throughout the rough terrain of the South American Andes mountain range. According to the Drug Enforcement Agency (DEA), what equivalent land area in South America does it take to grow enough coca to satisfy the United States' annual demand for cocaine?
    A. The state of Rhode Island
    B. A baseball field
    C. The borough of Queens, New York
    D. A K-mart parking lot

28. Working Americans with drug or alcohol problems are 25 percent less productive at their jobs than those without such problems. What percent of working Americans are impaired by some form of substance abuse problem?
    A. 15 percent
    B. 30 percent
    C. 20 percent
    D. 40 percent

29. Twenty-five percent of this group favors some form of decriminalization of marijuana.
    A. National Organization for Reform of Marijuana Laws (NORML)
    B. The drug gangs known as the Bloods or the Crips
    C. Colombian drug lords
    D. The nation's top chief prosecutors

30. At a cost of almost $100,000 to the taxpayer, 3,500 Customs Service employees were recently tested for illegal drugs. How many tested positive?
    A. 1
    B. 158
    C. 564
    D. 1,682

Note: Check your answers with the answer key at the back of the book.

LET'S LOOK AT ALCOHOL ON TV

The use of alcohol is portrayed in television programming as well as in advertising. Although portrayal of alcohol use in soap operas, movies, sitcoms, and dramas reflects societal use of alcohol, it also influences our images and attitudes about alcohol use. In this exercise, we ask you to watch five hours of television. It may be helpful to watch daytime soap operas as well as prime-time network programming. Write down the name of the program and its scheduled time. While you are viewing, consider the several questions: Is the portrayal of alcohol use responsible or irresponsible? Is it realistic?

Name of show:	Time:

Was the portrayal of alcohol use responsible or irresponsible? Was it realistic? Please explain.

Name of show:	Time:

Was the portrayal of alcohol use responsible or irresponsible? Was it realistic? Please explain.

Name of show:	Time:

Was the portrayal of alcohol use responsible or irresponsible? Was it realistic? Please explain.

Name of show:	Time:

Was the portrayal of alcohol use responsible or irresponsible? Was it realistic? Please explain.

Name of show:	Time:

Was the portrayal of alcohol use responsible or irresponsible? Was it realistic? Please explain.

Now that you have thought about TV's portrayal of alcohol use, think about the following question: Should television be held accountable for responsible and realistic portrayals of alcohol use in its programming? Now, your assignment is to write a letter to the president of a major network and advocate your position. If you believe television should be accountable, make suggestions of how the network might more effectively accomplish this task. If you do not believe television should be responsible for this, support your position.

DRUGS AND THE LAW

This survey has two parts. Both parts contain statements about possible consequences of being involved with illegal drugs. In the first part, mark the column that best describes how likely you think it is that the consequence described would occur. In the second part, mark the column that best describes how serious you think it would be if the consequence described occurred.

Part 1

		Very Likely	Likely	Not Sure	Unlikely	Very Unlikely
1.	If you were arrested with cocaine in your possession, how likely is it that you would serve a jail sentence?					
2.	If you were convicted of a drug-related felony, how likely is it that you would lose the right to vote?					
3.	If you had an arrest record for possession of a small amount of drugs, how likely is it to harm your career?					
4.	If you were with friends when they were arrested for having drugs, how likely is it that you would be arrested as well?					
5.	If you frequently use a false ID to obtain alcohol, how likely is it that you would be arrested?					
6.	If you are driving while intoxicated, how likely are you to get arrested?					
7.	If you regularly used illegal drugs, how likely is it you would eventually end up in legal trouble?					
8.	If you were put on probation for a drug offense, how likely do you think it is to cause serious problems in your life?					
9.	If you were taken to court for a drug offense, how likely is it you would lose most of your friends?					
10.	If you were arrested for a drug offense, how likely is it you would lose your job, even if you were not convicted?					

Part 2

		Very Serious	Serious	Not Sure	Somewhat Serious	Not Serious
11.	If you were convicted of possession of marijuana and given a fine and probation, how serious would it be?					
12.	If you were given a one-year jail sentence as the result of a drug conviction, how serious would it be?					
13.	If you lost your right to vote as a consequence of a felony drug conviction, how serious would it be?					
14.	If you were questioned by police or school authorities about drug activities, how serious would it be?					
15.	If you lost the right to travel outside of the United States as a consequence of a felony drug conviction, how serious would it be?					
16.	If on job applications, you had to reveal a conviction for cocaine possession, how serious do you think it would be?					
17.	If you were prevented from getting a civil service job because of a drug conviction, how serious would it be?					
18.	If police told your parents that you were associating with drug users, how serious would it be?					
19.	If a member of your family had to get you out of jail following a DWI arrest, how serious would it be?					
20.	If the police came to your house to ask about drug activities among your friends, how serious would it be?					

Note: Calculate your score using the instructions in the back of the book.

ALCOHOL IMAGES IN THE MEDIA: GOOD OR BAD?

Alcohol advertising can be some of the most sophisticated advertising in the business. When watching an advertisement, a viewer may not realize that the product manufacturer is trying to portray a certain image of the product shown. Media advertisements and the images they portray have come under increasing scrutiny by the public. The following exercise presents some issues in the debate over appropriate alcohol advertising at colleges and in society in general. What do you think? List both the pro and con sides of each issue presented. See if you can detect any patterns to your responses; if there are none, examine under what circumstances your opinions differ.

Alcohol Advertising at Colleges/Universities

Issue	Pro	Con
1. Sponsorship of college athletic events by alcohol beverage industry		
2. Alcohol advertising during televised college athletic events		
3. Spring break advertisements by alcohol companies		
4. Alcohol advertising in campus newspapers and on campus radio stations		

Alcohol Advertising in Society

Issue	Pro	Con
1. Alcohol advertising on television		
2. Use of attractive women in alcohol advertisements		
3. Use of sexual innuendo in alcohol advertising		
4. Public Service Announcements (PSAs) on responsible drinking by alcohol companies		

Additional Thoughts

These are just some of the issues surrounding alcohol advertisements and images portrayed in the media. Describe two additional issues not mentioned here.

What are your major disagreements, and/or concerns, regarding the use of the media in alcohol advertising?

In your opinion, what restrictions should be placed on the alcoholic beverage industry regarding the marketing of their products on college campuses and in the media?

SOCIETAL MYTHS ABOUT ALCOHOL AND OTHER DRUGS

As a society, we hold various myths about alcohol and drugs as well as about their users. These myths are used to rationalize our behavior and support our inaction when we are confronted with an alcohol- or drug-related problem. The following exercise is aimed at identifying common alcohol and drug myths, how these myths may be obstacles to action, and means of overcoming destructive myths

Here are two examples of myths.

You cannot become an alcoholic drinking only beer.

Addiction to heroin is much worse than addiction to alcohol.

1. Identify a myth you hold about alcohol or drugs, their use, or the users.

2. What are the consequences of this myth for your campus? For your broader community?

3. How is this myth an obstacle to action that would alleviate or avoid any of the identified consequences?

4. How can this myth be overcome?

WHERE DO YOU STAND: INDIVIDUAL RIGHTS VS. THE PUBLIC GOOD

In the United States, the Constitution protects individual rights including autonomy, protection of privacy, and freedom from undue governmental interference. In addition, policy decisions and governmental actions are also implemented to protect the public good. The public good is defined as the general health, well-being, and protection of the population. Occasionally, an issue presents itself that poses a conflict between individual rights and the public good. In the area of alcohol and drugs, several issues have emerged in recent years. These issues include implementation of DWI laws, law enforcement and interdiction of illicit drugs, the legal drinking age, needle exchange programs, and drug testing of individuals. Choose one of these topics, and respond to the following questions.

Topic ____

1. What are the individual's rights in this case?

2. How is the public good defined in this case?

3. Is there a conflict between individual rights and the public good?

4. How would you resolve this conflict? Why have you chosen the options you've identified?

5. What are the social, economic, and legal costs and benefits of your decision?

ADDRESSING CAMPUS ISSUES

On college campuses today, administrators are implementing new policies on alcohol and drug use. National chapters are placing tighter restrictions on alcohol consumption within fraternity and sorority houses, and some campuses are reconsidering regulations concerning alcohol use during rush activities. Yet, addressing alcohol and drug use on campuses is a complex task.

What are the rights and responsibilities of students regarding alcohol and drug use on campus?

What types of prevention activities can be effective on college and university campuses?

How can students work to ensure responsible alcohol use for legal drinkers?

This skill-building section attempts to assist you in developing the thought processes and skills necessary to achieve a comprehensive perspective on the problems of alcohol and other drug use on your campus. Some of the skills include assessing the impact of alcohol and drugs on your campus, developing problem-solving strategies to address drug and alcohol issues, and identifying existing and needed resources in your community.

ASSESSING THE IMPACT OF ALCOHOL AND DRUGS ON YOUR CAMPUS

The use of alcohol and drugs presents many challenges and dilemmas for every campus. Many campuses are considering new policies that may reflect a less permissive attitude. This exercise is designed to enable you to identify the impact of alcohol and drugs on your campus and to propose possible solutions for a problem you identify.

1. Identify the impact and problems connected to the use of alcohol and drugs on your campus. Identify as many issues/problems as you wish.

2. Prioritize your identified problems based on your assessment of their seriousness and importance.

3. Now choose one of those prioritized areas and go through the following steps:

a) Give a specific and concrete definition of the problem.

b) Who is impacted or affected by the problem?

c) Who enables or perpetuates the problem?

d) Who benefits from the problem?

e) What are the obstacles to change?

4. Propose a specific solution for this problem.

a) How would your solution be implemented?

b) How would you evaluate its effectiveness?

LEGAL ISSUES WITH SERVING ALCOHOL ON CAMPUS

Depending on state and local alcohol-related laws, event organizers and servers may be liable for injuries and damage caused by guests. Practices that may increase alcohol liability risks include:

- serving alcoholic beverages to obviously intoxicated persons
- serving alcoholic beverages to persons under 21 years of age
- mismanaging intoxicated persons

Students who host campus parties where alcoholic beverages are served are no different than any other servers. They have the responsibility of controlling who is and is not served alcohol at their events. Because alcohol-related laws and penalties vary among states, this exercise requires that you investigate the legal issues of serving alcohol on your campus. Use the following questions as a guide for learning about the laws in your area and how they affect campus parties where alcohol is served.

For this exercise, choose one of these categories, and investigate the answers for each question.

General Regulations (state or local area)

What is the legal minimum age to consume alcohol?

What is the legal age to serve alcohol? What is the legal age to sell alcohol?

What is the state blood alcohol content (BAC) limit for driving while intoxicated?

Does your state/county have specific laws regulating server training? If yes, what are they?

Server Liability

Does your state have Dram Shop Liability Laws, i.e., laws that explain the exact liability of a licensee, manager, bartender or server, should they violate the state liquor law?

If yes, what are the penalties associated with violation of these laws?

If your state does not have Dram Shop Liability Laws, are there common negligence laws or social host laws under which servers can still be held liable for serving minors or visibly intoxicated persons?

How do the Dram Shop or other liability laws affect campus organizations such as fraternity or sorority chapters, athletic teams, and student clubs?

Campus Regulations

In addition to state or local laws, colleges and universities may have their own campus regulations for hosting parties where alcohol is served.

Is a campus ID required for admission to parties where alcohol is served?

Is an age ID required for access to alcohol? If yes, what are some valid forms of identification?

Are procedures used to identify guests who are over 21 (e.g., wristbands)?

Is the self-service of alcohol prohibited?

Are non-drinking monitors required at parties where alcohol is served? If yes, do the monitors receive any training (e.g., responsible host or responsible service training)?

Is alcohol service stopped at least one hour before the event ends?

Student Organization Regulations

Some student organizations may create their own policies for hosting parties on campus. If you are involved in a campus student group, answer the following questions about your group's party policies:

Does your residence/organization have a written policy on alcohol service?

Do you discuss the policy and procedures at house/organization meetings at least once a semester?

Do all party planners follow the written guidelines?

Does your organization use servers and monitors at parties where alcohol is served?

Do servers follow a written job description that includes a requirement for training?

Do monitors follow a written job description that includes a requirement for training?

Does your organization assign monitors on the basis of number of guests at the party?

Do servers and monitors know the number of drinks required for men and women of various weights to reach legal intoxication?

Can servers and monitors state signs of intoxication?

Although parties are often used as a means for students to relax, have fun, and escape the pressures of academics, neither the host nor the guests can ignore their responsibilities for ensuring a safe party environment.

SOURCES: Ryan, B., Colthurst, T. & Segars, L. (1997). *College Alcohol Risk Assessment Guide: Environmental Approaches to Prevention.* Higher Education Center for Alcohol and Drug Prevention, US Department of Education.

Training for Intervention ProcedureS (TIPS) web page: http://www.gettips.com

INVESTIGATE THE DRUG AND ALCOHOL POLICY FOR YOUR CAMPUS

You have been nominated to serve on a committee established to review campus drug and alcohol policies. First, you must determine what policies currently exist.

1. What is the current policy on alcohol and drugs for your campus?

2. What groups or individuals does this policy address?

3. What issues does the policy address?

4. What rules, regulations, and penalties are included in this policy?

5. Is there anything in the policy you would change? If so, what would you change and why?

PREVENTION: WHAT IS IT?

Prevention efforts take many forms on college campuses, from drug and alcohol education classes to legal sanctions for use and possession. Several levels of prevention are appropriate and necessary if a prevention program is to be comprehensive.

Primary prevention is directed at individuals who have not yet tried alcohol and/or other drugs and has as its goal the prevention of use.

Secondary prevention is directed at individuals who are experimental users of alcohol and/or other drugs and has as its goal the prevention of abuse and addiction.

Tertiary prevention is directed at individuals who are addicted, and has intervention/treatment as its goals, and at individuals who are in recovery and has the prevention of relapse as its goal.

A comprehensive prevention program on a college campus may have several components including:

A. Educational component – provides facts and information.

B. Affective component – deals with attitudes, beliefs, and feelings.

C. Skill-building component – develops competencies such as assertiveness and decision-making.

D. Social support component – provides a social support network of students, faculty, and staff.

E. Social norms component - seeks to alter prevailing norms on use of alcohol or drugs.

F. Administrative component - provides policy guidelines for students and organizations.

G. Treatment component - provides access to appropriate screening and/or treatment programs.

WHAT WORKS IN PREVENTION

Colleges and universities have taken a variety of approaches to alcohol and drug use problems. Several of these are listed below. How effective do you believe each of the following approaches have been in preventing alcohol and other drug use problems among college students?

	Not at all Effective				Very Effective
1. Develop a tough administrative policy with severe penalties for anyone caught illegally using alcohol or other drugs.	1	2	3	4	5
2. Make written materials on the dangers of alcohol, tobacco, and other drug use available to all students, faculty, and staff.	1	2	3	4	5
3. Implement a year-round random drug testing program for students, faculty, and staff.	1	2	3	4	5
4. Provide training for faculty and staff on the health, legal, and ethical risks of alcohol, tobacco, and other drug use.	1	2	3	4	5
5. Provide opportunities for student groups (i.e., residence hall assistants, athletic teams, etc.) to discuss guidelines for the use and nonuse of alcohol and other drugs.	1	2	3	4	5
6. Provide opportunities for students to discuss the consequences of the health, legal, and ethical risks of alcohol, tobacco, and other drug use during freshman orientation.	1	2	3	4	5
7. Provide student leadership training aimed at preventing alcohol and other drug use.	1	2	3	4	5
8. Provide students with instructions and practice in personal and social skills to resist pressures to use alcohol and other drugs.	1	2	3	4	5
9. Assist students in planning and conducting alcohol and drug-free activities.	1	2	3	4	5
10. Conduct an annual alcohol awareness campaign on campus.	1	2	3	4	5
11. Conduct a public service announcement campaign to change how students think about drinking.	1	2	3	4	5
12. Develop a media campaign that focuses on the percentage of students who do not binge drink or abuse alcohol.	1	2	3	4	5
13. Bring in celebrities and recovering chemically dependent speakers to describe the consequences of alcohol and other drug use to students, faculty, and staff.	1	2	3	4	5

QUESTIONS

One of the challenges that many universities face is creating campus prevention programs that address alcohol use among both underage and legal age students.

1. Which of the above prevention approaches do you believe would be most effective in preventing alcohol use/abuse among underage students and why?

2. Which of the prevention approaches do you believe would be most effective in promoting responsible alcohol use among legal age students and why?

3. What effective prevention approaches are currently being used on your campus? What do you think makes them successful?

SOURCE: Adapted from *Policies and Programs for the 1990s:* Health Promotion Resources for U.S. Departments of Transportation, Education, and Health and Human Services (1990).

ALCOHOL AND DRUG ABUSE PREVENTION ON YOUR CAMPUS: WHAT DOES IT TAKE?

If you were in charge of developing a comprehensive alcohol and drug abuse prevention program for your campus, what would you do? List your goals, the activities you would use to achieve those goals, and the groups you would target for these activities.

	GOALS	ACTIVITIES	TARGET GROUPS
1.			
2.			
3.			
4.			

LET'S PARTY!

Parties on college campuses allow students to freely interact and put aside academic responsibilities for some relaxation. Some parties involve the heavy use of alcohol though, which can have negative consequences on students' health and well-being. Take time in this exercise to consider these questions in planning your party:

- What ingredients make up a successful party?
- What might occur at the party to make people inhibited?
- What might increase the danger of harm to students attending the party?
- How does a party atmosphere change people's behavior around sex?
- What steps can you take to create a safe atmosphere at your party?

The Campus Party Planning Guide offers suggestions for safe partying. Read it carefully and answer the questions that follow.

Campus Party Planning Guide: How to Keep the Party Alive

"Responsible drinking is drinking without harming oneself or those around you." This includes knowing one's limit, ensuring that drinking is not the primary activity, and obeying campus regulations. The following guidelines are offered to help promote safe partying and encourage the responsible use of alcohol among students.

Responsible Hosting Practices:

- Always serve food with alcohol. Drinking on an empty stomach is unwise (guests may get drunk faster and consume greater amounts of alcohol).
- Always make mixed drinks as they are to be made (i.e., follow the recipe).
- Always offer non-alcoholic beverages. This is common courtesy.
- If you serve an alcohol punch, make it with a non-carbonated base. The body absorbs alcohol faster when it is mixed with something carbonated.
- Never force anyone to drink alcohol.
- Don't encourage the gulping or "chugging" of drinks. Guests may become intoxicated and could even pass out.
- Plan activities for the party that do not involve alcohol. There should be something else besides drinking to do at the gathering (e.g., dancing).
- Make sure your guests understand your expectations regarding their drinking behavior. Make contingency plans for those who drink too much.

You can model responsible drinking behavior for your guests by offering the following tips and of course, you should practice them yourself!

Responsible Drinking Practices:

- Set a limit on the number of drinks you will have at any function and stick to it.
- Drink slowly. Don't gulp or chug your drinks. Allow yourself no more than one drink/hour.
- Go light! Dilute your drinks with juice or water, but avoid carbonated mixers.
- Know what is in your drink: avoid "everything goes" punches and watch while your drink is prepared.
- Don't drink on an empty stomach. Eat high protein foods such as cheese or meat before drinking.

- Never allow yourself to be pressured into "just one more drink" or "one for the road."
- Set a time to leave the party or event and stick to it.
- Don't encourage or reinforce inappropriate or irresponsible drinking behavior.
- Decide why you drink. Respect a person who chooses not to drink.
- Periodically reassess your own drinking behavior and attitude toward alcohol.
- Engage in responsible drinking behavior that your fellow students can emulate.

QUESTIONS

What barriers exist to following the suggestions of this guide?

What advantages exist to following this guide?

How might you change the guide?

SOURCE: Adapted from "How to Keep the Party Alive." Peer Health Advocate Norm Misperceptions Peer Module, Fall 1994: Everyone is Doing It, Are You? Project Aware: Alcohol and Drug Awareness and Prevention Education. SUNY Cortland, Cortland NY. Funded by FIPSE, US Department of Education.

WHERE CAN I FIND HELP?

On your campus and within the broader community, numerous resources exist to assist those who may be concerned about their own or a family member's alcohol or drug use. However, we are often unaware of them. This exercise will facilitate your awareness of community resources and foster an appreciation for the process of the individual who is seeking help for an alcohol or drug problem. You can obtain a list of potential resources/services on campus and within the community through your campus health center, campus counseling center, residence-hall advisors, local health department offices, and the telephone directory under alcohol/drug addiction treatment services or mental health services. Once you have chosen a service, contact them by telephone to set up an appointment. By obtaining answers to the following items, you will have basic information about the services/resources. Feel free to ask other questions and note your questions with the responses on the following interview sheet.

Agency/Office:

Address:

Phone:

Hours:

Contact Person:

Fees:

Services Offered:

Intake Procedure/How do you access services:

Agency Philosophy on Alcohol/Drugs:

Other Comments:

IN SUMMARY

Hopefully, with the completion of this workbook, you have become more aware and sensitized to the effects that alcohol and other drugs have on you personally, in your relationships, and in your community.

This final section helps you to synthesize and integrate the insights you have gained. The *Personal Reflections* exercise asks you to summarize what you have learned about yourself. The *Personal Risk for Addiction* questionnaire forces you to take a critical look at your potential for developing chemical dependence. Finally, the *Intentions* survey requires you to commit to paper your willingness to become actively involved in the struggle to overcome drug and alcohol problems in our society.

PERSONAL REFLECTIONS

Congratulations! You have completed *Making Choices.* You have given lots of thought to your own behavior, feelings, and thoughts; your relationships; and your views of the world around you. Based on the self assessment exercises in *Making Choices,* it is time to summarize what you have learned about yourself. The following series of questions will help you integrate and synthesize what you have learned. Take your time and freely refer back through the exercises to help you respond.

1. Has your awareness of your alcohol/drug use changed? If so, how?

2. What factors have you identified as having an impact on your use?

3. Do you have any specific concerns about yourself or someone close to you? How will you address those concerns?

4. Assess your level of risk-taking behavior with regard to alcohol/drugs. Are you comfortable with your level of risk-taking? If not, how would you change ?

5. Have you altered your ways of coping with stress or using your leisure time? If so, how?

6. Have any of your attitudes toward alcohol or drugs changed? If so, how have they changed?

PERSONAL RISK FOR ADDICTION

Based on your responses to the exercises in this workbook and your increased self-awareness, circle each of the following characteristics that you believe apply to you.

1. I use alcohol or other drugs on a regular basis.
2. I have experienced some negative consequences or problems as a result of my alcohol or drug use.
3. I have a family history (grandparent, parent, or sibling) of chemical dependence (including alcoholism).
4. I tend to have a compulsive personality.
5. I worry or feel bad about my alcohol or drug use.
6. I have friends who use alcohol or other drugs on a regular basis.

Score _______________ (total number circled)

If you circled 2 or more of these items, you are at increased risk for addiction, as compared to the general public. It may be useful for you to seek the guidance of a counselor trained to assist with drug and alcohol problems. Please do not take the results of this lightly, it could mean your life.

INTENTIONS

All of us have a role to play in our society's struggle to overcome drug and alcohol problems. In some cases, our role is to focus on our own relationship with alcohol and other drugs. For others, it is dealing with the chemical dependence of a family member or close friend. Still others play a role in campus and community prevention and treatment efforts.

What is your role?

List below your intentions to get involved. You can get involved on a personal level, a relationship level, a community level, or all three.

<u>On a personal level</u>

I intend to ...

<u>In my relationships</u>

I intend to ...

<u>On my campus</u>

I intend to ...

<u>In my community</u>

I intend to ...

ANSWERS AND SCORING INSTRUCTIONS

PHYSICAL EFFECTS OF ALCOHOL USE

Item No.	Correct Answer	Item No.	Correct Answer
1.	F	11.	T
2.	F	12.	F
3.	T	13.	T
4.	T	14.	T
5.	T	15.	F
6.	F	16.	T
7.	F	17.	F
8.	F	18.	F
9.	T	19.	F
10.	T	20.	T

This assessment should be scored by counting the number of correct answers. Items marked "**Don't Know**" or left blank should be scored as incorrect.

Number Correct	Rating
18 or greater	Excellent
16-17	Very Good
14-15	Good
12-13	Fair
Less than 12	Poor

PHYSICAL CONSEQUENCES OF DRUG USE

Item No.	Correct Answer	Item No.	Correct Answer
1.	T	9.	T
2.	F	10.	T
3.	T	11.	F
4.	T	12.	T
5.	F	13.	F
6.	F	14.	F
7.	T	15.	T
8.	F		

This assessment should be scored by counting the number of correct answers. Items marked "**Don't Know**" or left blank should be scored as incorrect.

Number Correct	Rating
14 or greater	Excellent
12-13	Good
10-11	Fair
Less than 10	Poor

IDEAS ABOUT ALCOHOL USE

Point values are assigned to response options as follows:

Item No.	Strongly Agree	Agree	Not Sure	Disagree	Strongly Disagree
1.	1	2	3	4	5
2.	1	2	3	4	5
3.	1	2	3	4	5
4.	5	4	3	2	1
5.	5	4	3	2	1
6.	5	4	3	2	1
7.	5	4	3	2	1
8.	1	2	3	4	5
9.	5	4	3	2	1
10.	5	4	3	2	1
11.	1	2	3	4	5
12.	1	2	3	4	5
13.	5	4	3	2	1
14.	5	4	3	2	1
15.	5	4	3	2	1
16.	1	2	3	4	5
17.	1	2	3	4	5
18.	5	4	3	2	1
19.	1	2	3	4	5
20.	1	2	3	4	5

This inventory should be scored by adding the point values of the responses from all of the questions and dividing this total by 20. The maximum attainable score of five points indicates you believe using alcohol can be detrimental to your social, emotional, and physical well-being. A minimum score of one indicates you believe using alcohol can enhance your social, emotional, and physical well-being.

My Score is: ____________________ $\frac{\text{(Total Points)}}{20}$

IDEAS ABOUT DRUG USE

Point values are assigned to responses as follows:

Item No.	Strongly Agree	Agree	Not Sure	Disagree	Strongly Disagree
1.	5	4	3	2	1
2.	5	4	3	2	1
3.	1	2	3	4	5
4.	1	2	3	4	5
5.	1	2	3	4	5
6.	5	4	3	2	1
7.	5	4	3	2	1
8.	1	2	3	4	5
9.	1	2	3	4	5
10.	1	2	3	4	5
11.	1	2	3	4	5
12.	5	4	3	2	1
13.	5	4	3	2	1
14.	1	2	3	4	5
15.	1	2	3	4	5
16.	5	4	3	2	1
17.	5	4	3	2	1
18.	1	2	3	4	5
19.	5	4	3	2	1
20.	1	2	3	4	5

This inventory should be scored by adding the point values of the responses from all questions. Divide this total by 20. The maximum attainable score of five points indicates you believe using illegal drugs is detrimental to your social, emotional, and physical well-being. A minimum score of one indicates you believe using illegal drugs can enhance your social, emotional, and physical well-being.

My Score is: __________ $\frac{\text{(Total Points)}}{20}$

HAVE A DRINK?

Point values are assigned to response options as follows:

Definitely Yes	=	5
Probably Yes	=	4
Maybe	=	3
Probably No	=	2
Definitely No	=	1

This inventory should be scored by adding the point values of all your responses and dividing the total by 20. The maximum attainable score of 5 indicates you are strongly tempted to drink in a wide variety of situations. A score in the mid-range of 3 indicates that under some circumstances you may be tempted to drink. A low score around 1 indicates you are rarely tempted to drink regardless of the situation.

My Score is:____________ $\frac{\text{(Total Points)}}{20}$

WOULD YOU AVOID DRUGS?

Point values are assigned to responses as follows:

Very confident	=	5
Confident	=	4
Somewhat Confident	=	3
Not Very Confident	=	2
Not At All Confident	=	1

This inventory should be scored by adding the point values of all your responses and dividing the total by 15. The result is your average perceived ability to avoid drug use in general. The maximum attainable score of 5 points indicates a strong perceived ability to avoid using drugs. A minimum score of 1 indicates little or no perceived ability to avoid using drugs.

My Score is: ____________ (Total Points) / 15

WHY DO YOU SMOKE?

Write the number you have circled after each statement in the corresponding space below. Add the scores down each column to get your totals. For example, the sum of your scores for A, G, and M gives you the total score for the first column.

	A ____	B ____	C ____	D ____	E ____	F ____
	G ____	H ____	I ____	J ____	K ____	L ____
	M ____	N ____	O ____	P ____	Q ____	R ____
Column Totals	1 ____	2 ____	3 ____	4 ____	5 ____	6 ____
	Stimulation	Handling	Pleasure	Crutch	Craving	Habit

In this test, a score of 11 or above on any factor indicates that smoking is an important source of satisfaction for you. The higher your score (15 is the highest), the more important a particular factor is in your smoking and the more useful the discussion of that factor can be in your attempt to quit. If you do not score high on any of the six factors, you, more than likely, do not smoke very much or have not been smoking for very many years. If so, giving up smoking—and staying off—should be easy.

The following categories describe motivations for smoking and suggest alternative activities to meet those needs.

1. Stimulation

If you score high or fairly high on this factor, you are one of those smokers who is stimulated by the cigarette—you feel that it helps to wake you up, organize your energies, and keep you going. If you try to give up smoking, you may want a safe substitute, such as a brisk walk or moderate exercise, whenever you feel the urge to smoke.

2. Handling

Handling things can be satisfying, but there are many ways to keep your hands busy without lighting up or playing with a cigarette. Why not toy with a pen or pencil? Or try doodling. Or play with a coin, a piece of jewelry, or some other harmless object.

3. Accentuation of Pleasure—Pleasurable Relaxation

It is not always easy to determine whether you use the cigarette to feel *good*, that is, get real, honest pleasure out of smoking (Factor 3), or to keep from feeling *bad* (Factor 4). About two-thirds of smokers score high or fairly high on *accentuation of pleasure*, and about half of those also score as high or higher on *reduction of negative feelings*. Those who do get real pleasure out of smoking often find that honest consideration of the harmful effects of their habit is enough to help them quit. They substitute social and physical activities and find they do not seriously miss their cigarettes.

4. Reduction of Negative Feelings, or "Crutch"

Many smokers use cigarettes as a kind of crutch in moments of stress or discomfort. But the heavy smoker, the person who tries to handle severe personal problems by smoking many times a day, is apt to discover that cigarettes do not help in dealing with problems effectively. When it comes to quitting, this kind of smoker may find it easy to stop when everything is going well, but may be tempted to start again in a time of crisis. Again, physical exertion or social activity may serve as useful substitutes for cigarettes, even in times of tension.

5. "Craving" or Dependence

Quitting smoking is difficult for the person who scores high on this factor. For the addicted smoker, the craving for a cigarette begins to build up the moment the cigarette is put out, so tapering off is not likely to work. This smoker must go "cold turkey." If you are dependent on cigarettes, it may be helpful for you to smoke more than usual for a day or two, so that the taste for cigarettes is spoiled. Then isolate yourself completely from cigarettes until the craving is gone.

6. Habit

If you are smoking out of habit, you no longer get much satisfaction from your cigarettes. You just light them frequently without even realizing you are doing so. You may find it easy to quit and stay off if you can break the habit patterns you have created. Cutting down gradually may be quite effective if there is a change in the way the cigarettes are smoked and the conditions under which they are smoked. The key to success is to become aware of each cigarette you smoke. This can be done by asking yourself, "Do I really want this cigarette?" You may be surprised at how many you do not want.

You must make two important decisions: 1) whether to go without the satisfactions you get from smoking or find an appropriate, less hazardous substitute activity, and 2) whether to cut out cigarettes all at once, or taper off. Your scores on this test should guide you in making these decisions.

COPING STRATEGIES

Categories of coping responses:

Numbers	Type of Response
1, 5, 9, 11, 19	Relaxation — did something with the intent of relaxing (besides #1, a large number of "yes" answers to these other statements may point to problems with excessive use of alcohol and other drugs).
4, 7, 26, 30, 39	Social support — sought or found emotional support from loved ones, friends, or professionals.
2, 8, 13, 25, 36	Spiritual — sought or found spiritual comfort and support.
6, 21, 27, 29, 35	Resignation — accepted that the problem had occurred, but nothing could be done about it.
16, 20, 22, 32, 34	Cognitive reappraisal — tried to see the problem in a different light that made it seem more bearable.
10, 14, 18, 33, 37	Problem-solving strategies — thought about solutions to the problem, gathered information about it, or actually did something to try to solve it.
12, 23, 28, 31, 38	Self-expression — expressed emotions in response to the problem to reduce tension, anxiety, or frustration
3, 15, 17, 24, 40	Diversion — diverted attention away from the problem by thinking about other things or engaging in some activity.

ARE YOU A RISK TAKER?

Risks can be classified into several categories.

Numbers	Type of Risk
5, 7, 8, 9, 10, 13	Social — are those you take in interpersonal relationships and/or in social situations for example, attending a party where you do not know anyone.
1, 2, 3, 4, 11	Physical — are those that expose you to possible bodily harm, like sky diving.
18, 20	Intellectual — are those that may reveal your lack of knowledge or inability to perform mental tasks.
6, 12, 16, 17	Emotional — are those that may expose you to emotional pain or hurt feelings.
15, 19	Financial — are those that expose you to possible monetary or property losses.

LEISURE INTEREST CHECKLIST

Totals

Count up the total for each of the following categories:

Total number of strong interests.. ______

Total number of activities in which you are currently participating............ ______

Total number of activities during which you might use alcohol or other drugs.. ______

Total number of activities you would like to try in the future.................. ______

ARE YOU PROTECTED?: RISK AND RESILIENCY FACTORS

Add up your points based upon your answers. Subtract the negative scores from the positive scores to produce a total score.

If you answered to Question #	YES	NO
1.	3	-3
2.	3	-3
3.	3	-3
4.	5	-5
5.	-3	3
6.	5	-5
7.	3	-3
8.	3	-3
9.	-3	3
10.	3	-3
11.	-3	3
12.	-3	3
13.	-3	3
14.	-3	3
15.	3	-3

TOTAL SCORE:____________________ (cont'd on next page)

INTERPRETATION:

If your total score is a negative number, then your risk factors for developing an alcohol or other drug problem outweigh your protective factors and you could be at risk. If your total score is a positive number, then your protective factors outweigh your risk factors for developing an alcohol or other drug problem and you are probably at low risk. The larger the number is in either direction (positive or negative) the more significant the results. For example, a large negative number (i.e., -35) would indicate significant risk for developing an alcohol or other drug problem. A large positive number (i.e., +35) would indicate a relatively high level of protective factors and minimal risk of developing an alcohol or other drug problem.

LIFE SATISFACTION QUESTIONNAIRE

Add up your circled responses and divide by 30.

INTERPRETATION OF SCORES

This scale measures how satisfied you are with the various aspects of your life. High scores indicate a high degree of satisfaction. If you scored lower than 3.0, you indicated dissatisfaction with various aspects of your life. If you scored above 3.0, you indicated satisfaction with many aspects of your life. Look at those items in which you responded with a 2 or less. Those are the aspects of your life with which you are particularly dissatisfied.

No one of us can be expected to be satisfied with every particular aspect of our lives. In interpreting your scores, you probably found some areas of your life about which you feel very satisfied and others about which you feel very unsatisfied. That is quite natural. There is always something that can be done to either improve an aspect of your life so you are less dissatisfied with it, or employ some strategies to feel better about those aspects of your life that cannot be changed.

FRIENDS

Point values are assigned to responses as follows:

Item Number	All of My Friends	Most of My Friends	Some of My Friends	A Few of My Friends	None of My Friends
1	5	4	3	2	1
2	1	2	3	4	5
3	5	4	3	2	1
4	5	4	3	2	1
5	5	4	3	2	1
6	1	2	3	4	5
7	5	4	3	2	1
8	5	4	3	2	1
9	1	2	3	4	5
10	1	2	3	4	5

This inventory should be scored by adding the point values of all your responses and dividing the total by 10. The maximum attainable score of 5 points indicates you perceive your friends to be opposed to illegal or irresponsible drug use. A mid-range score of 3 indicates you have some friends who are opposed to drug use and some who accept it. A minimum score of 1 suggests you perceive your friends to be accepting or encouraging of illegal or irresponsible drug use.

My Score is:____________ $\frac{\text{(Total Points)}}{10}$

WHAT DO MY PARENTS THINK?

Point values are assigned to responses as follows:

Item Number	Definitely Yes	Probably Yes	Uncertain	Probably No	Definitely No
1.	1	2	3	4	5
2.	5	4	3	2	1
3.	5	4	3	2	1
4.	1	2	3	4	5
5.	5	4	3	2	1
6.	1	2	3	4	5
7.	5	4	3	2	1
8.	1	2	3	4	5
9.	5	4	3	2	1
10.	5	4	3	2	1

This inventory should be scored by adding the point values of all your responses and dividing the total by 10. The maximum attainable score of 5 points indicates you perceive your parents to be opposed to illegal or irresponsible drug use. A mid-range score of 3 indicates you perceive your parents to be inconsistent or uncertain about their attitudes towards alcohol or drug use. A minimum score of 1 suggests you perceive your parents to be accepting of illegal or irresponsible drug use.

HOW HEALTHY IS YOUR FAMILY?

For each correct answer, give yourself one point:

1.	true	4.	false	7.	true	10.	false
2.	true	5.	false	8.	true	11.	false
3.	true	6.	false	9.	true	12.	false

10-12 points — means you are very lucky to be part of a healthy and functional family.

4-9 points — means you have a family that tends to be functional but has some unhealthy characteristics.

1-3 points — means you have a family that is dysfunctional and unhealthy. Alcoholism, drug abuse, physical/sexual abuse may also be present. Professional help is seriously recommended.

ALCOHOL USE AND SEXUALITY

1. TRUE: Alcohol use is a very strong predictor of rape particularly when both individuals have been drinking (Avis, H., 1996, Drugs and Life, 3rd Edition. Madison, WI: Brown and Benchmark Publishers).

2. TRUE: (Higher Education Center for Alcohol and Other Drug Prevention, Alcohol and Acquaintance Rape: Strategies to Protect Yourself and Each Other. U.S. Department of Education Pub. No. ED/OPE 96-6).

3. TRUE: Approximately 1 out of every 6 college women are victims of acquaintance rape or attempted rape every year (Higher Education Center for Alcohol and Other Drug Prevention, Alcohol and Acquaintance Rape: Strategies to Protect Yourself and Each Other. U.S. Department of Education Pub. No. ED/OPE 96-6).

4. TRUE: (Higher Education Center for Alcohol and Other Drug Prevention, Alcohol and Acquaintance Rape: Strategies to Protect Yourself and Each Other. U.S. Department of Education Pub. No. ED/OPE 96-6).

5. FALSE: Alcohol use impairs judgment due to its effect on the brain. This often prevents the individual from making rational choices about his or her sexual behavior. As a result, individuals who drink, use condoms less frequently than those who do not drink (Carroll, C.R., 1996, Drugs in Modern Society, 4th Edition Madison, WI: Brown and Benchmark Publishers).

6. TRUE: Sex under the influence of alcohol can result in unwanted pregnancy and sexually transmitted diseases, including AIDS. This is due in part to decreased judgment, decreased likelihood of using condoms, and the effects of alcohol on the immune system (Carroll, C.R., 1996, Drugs in Modern Society, 4th Edition. Madison, WI: Brown and Benchmark Publishers).

7. FALSE: Alcohol use may lead to an increase in perceived sexual arousal, but in actuality, alcohol causes a decrease in strength of erection, decreased vaginal lubrication and decreased orgasmic response (Avis, H., 1996, Drugs and Life, 3rd Edition. Madison, WI: Brown and Benchmark Publishers).

8. TRUE: In a national study, approximately half of college binge drinkers reported that they engaged in unplanned sexual activity. This is due, in part, to an inability to communicate their desires when under the influence of alcohol (Avis, H., 1996, Drugs and Life, 3rd Edition. Madison, WI: Brown and Benchmark Publishers).

THE EFFECTS OF THE USE OF ALCOHOL AND OTHER DRUGS ON SOCIETY

Correct Responses

1. b	11. c	21. a
2. a	12. c	22. d
3. b	13. b	23. d
4. a	14. b	24. b
5. a	15. a	25. a
6. c	16. a	26. a
7. c	17. c	27. c
8. b	18. a	28. a
9. a	19. c	29. d
10. c	20. c	30. a

Add up all of your correct responses.

27 - 30 Good score! You are well informed on issues surrounding drug and alcohol use in society.

24 - 26 Give yourself a pat on the back; you are well aware of some of the negative effects alcohol and drug use can have on society.

21 - 23 Not bad; you are on your way to realizing the dangerous effects alcohol and drug use can have on society overall.

18 - 20 Needs some work; you are not fully cognizant of the impact of alcohol and drug use on our society.

Below 18 Time to get informed about some of the issues associated with drug and alcohol use in society.

Score Part 1, the Likelihood Scale, and Part 2, the Seriousness Scale separately.

Part 1 - The Likelihood Scale

Point values are assigned to responses as follows:

Very Likely	=	5
Likely	=	4
Not Sure	=	3
Unlikely	=	2
Very Unlikely	=	1

Add up the point values of all your responses, and divide the total by 10. The maximum attainable score of 5 points indicates you perceive a high likelihood that negative legal consequences could result from illegal drug use. A mid-range score of 3 indicates you are unsure about the probability of negative legal consequences. A minimum score of 1 suggests you perceive a low likelihood that negative legal consequences could result from illegal drug use.

Part 2 - The Seriousness Scale

Point values are assigned to responses as follows:

Very Serious	=	5
Serious	=	4
Not Sure	=	3
Somewhat Serious	=	2
Not Serious	=	1

Add the point values of all your responses, and divide the total by 10. The maximum attainable score of 5 points indicates you perceive the potential consequences of illegal drug use to be very serious. A mid-range score of 3 indicates you are unsure about the seriousness of these consequences. A minimum score of 1 suggests you perceive the potential consequences of illegal drug use to be not serious at all.

READ MORE ABOUT IT

Alcohol and Drugs

Carroll, C.R. 2000. Drugs in Modern Society (5th edition). Dubuque, IA: McGraw-Hill Publishers.

Fields, R. 1998. Drugs in Perspective (3rd edition). Dubuque, IA: McGraw-Hill Publishers.

Goldberg, R. 2000. Taking Sides: Clashing Views on Controversial Issues in Drugs and Society (4th edition). Burr Ridge, IL: McGraw-Hill Publishers.

Johnson, Vernon E. 1986. Intervention: How to Help Someone Who Doesn't Want Help. Minneapolis, MN: Johnson Institute.

Johnson, Vernon E. 1980. I'll Quit Tomorrow. New York, NY: Harper and Row, Publishers.

Kinney, J. 2000. Loosening the Grip - A Handbook of Alcohol Information (6th edition). Dubuque, IA: McGraw-Hill Publishers.

Palfai, T. and Jankiewicz, H. 1991. Drugs and Human Behavior. Dubuque, IA: Wm. C. Brown Publishers.

Ray, O. & Ksir C. 1999. Drugs, Society, & Human Behavior (8th edition). Dubuque, IA: McGraw-Hill Publishers.

Resnik, H. 1990. Youth and Drugs: Society's Mixed Messages. Rockville, MD: Office of Substance Abuse Prevention, Department of Health and Human Services.

Vaillant, G. E. 1983. The Natural History of Alcoholism. Cambridge, MA.: Harvard University Press.

Weil, A. 1986. The Natural Mind: An Investigation of Drugs and the Higher Consciousness. Boston, MA: Houghton Mifflin Company.

Wilson, H. 1999. Annual Editions: Drugs, Society, and Behavior 99/00 (14th edition). Burr Ridge, IL: McGraw-Hill Publishers.

Stress

Allen, R. J. and Hyde, D. H. 1988. Investigations in Stress Control. Edina, MN: Burgess International Group, Inc.

Benson, Herbert. 1975. The Relaxation Response. New York, NY: Avon Books.

Greenberg, J. 1999. Comprehensive Stress Management (6th edition). Dubuque, IA: McGraw-Hill Publishers.

Adult Children of Alcoholics

Black, C. 1981. It Will Never Happen to Me. Denver, CO: M.A.C. Printing and Publication Division.

Cermack, Timmen L. 1988. A Time to Heal: The Road to Recovery for Adult Children of Alcoholics. Los Angeles, CA: Jeremy P. Tarcher, Inc.

Seixas, J. S. & Youcha, G. 1985. Children of Alcoholism: A Survivor's Manual. New York, NY: Harper and Row Publishers.

Woititz, Janet. 1983. Adult Children of Alcoholics. Pompano Beach, FL: Health Communications, Inc.

RESOURCES ON THE WEB

The Higher Education Center for Alcohol and Other Drug Prevention
http://www.edc.org/hec

National Clearinghouse for Alcohol and Drug Information
http://www.health.org

National Council on Alcohol and Drug Dependence
http://www.ncadd.org

Center for Substance Abuse Prevention (CSAP)
http://www.coresoft.com/csap.html

Virtual Clearinghouse on Alcohol, Tobacco, and Other Drugs
http://www.ccsa.ca/atod.htm

National Center on Addiction & Substance Abuse (CASA/Columbia University)
http://www.casacolumbia.org

Promising Practices - Campus Alcohol Strategies
http://www.promprac.gmu.edu

BACCHUS/GAMMA Peer Education networks
http://www.linkmag.com/bacchus

Training for Intervention ProcedureS (TIPS)
http://www.gettips.com

Harvard School of Public Health College Alcohol Study
http://hsph.harvard.edu/cas

National Institute on Alcohol Abuse and Alcoholism
http://www.niaaa.nih.gov

National Institute on Drug Abuse
http://www.nida.nih.gov

Al-Anon
http://www.al-anon.org

Healthfinder
http://www.healthfinder.gov

Drugs Awareness Online: Use, Abuse, & Treatment
http://www.mhhe.com/hper/health/drugs

ABOUT THE AUTHORS

Sandra Crouse Quinn is an Assistant Professor in the Department of Health Behavior and Health Education in the School of Public Health, University of North Carolina at Chapel Hill. She currently teaches two graduate classes in community health education and conducts research in the area of HIV/AIDS. Prior to her doctoral training, she was a therapist in substance abuse treatment programs, employee assistance programs, and in private practice for 11 years. She designed and taught HLTH 498, Special Topics in Health: Personal and Community Perspectives on Alcohol and Drug Use, at the University of Maryland, College Park.

Marjorie E. Scaffa is an Associate Professor and Chairperson of the Department of Occupational Therapy at the University of South Alabama in Mobile. She received a Ph.D. in Health Education from the University of Maryland and a Master in Science degree in Occupational Therapy from Virginia Commonwealth University. Dr. Scaffa has worked in a number of clinical and community settings, including the National Institutes of Health, with individuals addicted to alcohol and other drugs, and their families. She has taught a variety of alcohol and drug courses at the University of Maryland, and is currently the Vice President of the Mental Health Association of Southwest Alabama. Her research interests include community mental health and substance abuse prevention.

Janice K. Ruffini is a Community Services Specialist with the Lee County Health Department in North Carolina. She received a Master of Public Health degree in Health Behavior and Health Education from the University of North Carolina at Chapel Hill. Her experience and career interests are based in college health education with a focus on substance abuse prevention. For her Master's thesis, she analyzed data from the CORE Alcohol and Drug Survey conducted at the University of Rochester in New York.